Oklahoma Horizons Series

Oklahoma Horizons Series

Oklahoma Heritage Association, Inc.
Oklahoma Heritage Publications Committee, 1994

INDOMITABLE OKLAHOMA WOMEN

Oklahoma Horizons Series

INDOMITABLE
OKLAHOMA WOMEN

by
Opal Hartsell Brown

Series Editor: Kenny A. Franks

Published for the Oklahoma Heritage Association
by Western Heritage Books

OTHER BOOKS BY OPAL HARTSELL BROWN

Loose Nuts on the Wheel (1963).
The Cross, the Cow or the Prayer Rug? (1970).
Murray County — Heart of Eden (1977).
City of Many Facets, with Richard Garrity, photographer (1981).
Nightshades of Haran (1984).
Classroom Challengers — 5s to 50s: The Woos and Woes of a Teacher, 1927-1972 (1990).

Manufactured in the United States of America for the Oklahoma Heritage Association, Oklahoma City.

ISBN: 0-86546-088-4

DEDICATION...

To women everywhere, especially those in Oklahoma,
and more especially to my mother, Nannie Herndon Hartsell,
a native of Indian Territory who was part Cherokee.
She could do anything from playing the organ
to manufacturing soap, including the lye. She
could bale hay or serve as a midwife for women and animals.
All these things and much more she did without title,
remuneration, or notable gratitude...until now.

INTRODUCTION

Modern women, who think they broke the male barrier to the work force and commerce, need to study the history of their forebears. In the words of the Chinese leader, Mao Tse Tung, "Women hold up half the sky." They always have. The main precept of this book is to show it.

Women were hunters and gatherers, tillers of the soil, harvesters and preservers, manufacturers, builders, doctors, nurses, scientists, teachers, ministers, and entertainers. These and numerous other services were duties of womanhood. Their homes were their bases of operation.

Women operated without license and generally without titles. Most of them received little, if any, monetary rewards or credit. The Bible and anthropology are excellent sources of information on this subject. The situation remained much the same until the Industrial Revolution and the establishment of public schools. These events drew many operations outside the homes. Women followed.

Confining the issue to Oklahoma, this book begins with the first homesteaders and proceeds to the present. Several women gained considerable recognition: Mrs. Walter Ferguson, Kate Bernard, Perle Mesta, Lucille Mulhall, Alice Robertson. A few of the noted ones are featured herein. Most of them, however, have lived and served unperceived, because their contributions were not sensational.

CONTENTS

ILLUSTRATIONS

INDOMITABLE OKLAHOMA WOMEN

Chapter I
HOMESTEADERS

DORA (DORAH) BELLE PRUITT BILES
(1872-1954)
Among the Throngs of Runners

Dora (Dorah) Belle Pruitt Biles was among the throngs of women who rumbled west in wagon trains during the 1800s. The new bride of George Hudson Thomas Biles, she was filled with romance and excitement when the wagon train ground out of Missouri and entered the chaos of swiftly changing Indian Territory. The travelers were going to California in search of riches.[1] Days grew longer over rough trails and across treacherous streams. The group worried about possible Indian attacks, as the dust became thicker and the heat more oppressive. Camping lost its luster and turned to drudgery.

A short distance into the Territory, the travelers heard of an impending run for land. At Fort Reno, people were already gathering for the event. Hundreds of men, women, and children milled around their covered wagons, tents, and animals. Some were cooking and eating, some were feeding animals and repairing vehicles, while others squatted in groups spinning yarns.[2] Dora's group replenished their supplies and rocked on two more weeks. Their water supply gave out. They and their animals suffered. "Bones of previous travelers and animals lay stretched and gaping in the sun and dust." An Indian man warned the travelers that there was no water ahead. They decided to return to Fort Reno and wait for the land run to be held on April 22, 1889.[3]

Back at the fort they made camp and plans. The women, children, and elderly members of the train formed one group to make the scheduled run. The younger, adventurous men became "Sooners." Avoiding the soldiers on guard, the adventurers made daily trips into the reserve to study the landscape and locate choice plots of 160 acres. Prior to the appointed hour to start, they hid in creeks and bushes.[4]

At the sound of the bugle or shots, they dashed from their hiding places and planted stakes for claims. Dora and her husband wound up with land where the city of El Reno now stands. Like many other new settlers, however, they did not like fading

into nature and becoming a part of it. Dora, especially, was disillusioned.[5] The daughter of a lawyer and teacher in Forsyth, Missouri, she had lived as convenient a life as cities had to offer in those days. Therefore she and her husband moved into Oklahoma City and opened a delicatessen. That meant hard work ten to twelve hours a day, 365 days a year.

Still desiring land, Dora's husband George made the run of 1891 into the Sac-Fox, Iowa, Pottawatomie, and Shawnee lands and got what he wanted. It was in Lincoln County. The Biles' first home was a half dugout—half of the crude structure above ground and half below. The top was made of logs.[6]

Clearing and breaking the land, planting and plowing, harvesting the yields, and preserving them continued day-in and day-out. Winter arrived. The family increased. The Biles needed a larger and better shelter. They would build a house. When a family got ready to build in those days, the neighbors gathered at the site for a house-raising or barn-raising. They cut and hewed the logs or lumber, hauled it to the location, and went to work.[7] When

Below: Among the thousands of women who braved the world of homesteaders in the Indian Territory during the 1800s was Dora Belle Pruitt Biles. Shown above holding her baby, Dora bore her first child at age seventeen and her fourteenth at age fifty. Her husband, George H. Biles, is second from left, front row. The couple raised several other children besides their own. (Courtesy Ruby Biles Wilson)

the building was finished, they all turned to feasting, visiting, and often dancing.

Life was hard for Dora, as it was for most women on the frontier, but her rewards were worth the sacrifice. By the age of fifty she had fourteen children. They grew to be noteworthy citizens. Those who entered the field of education served from Grove to Altus. One of them became Oklahoma highway commissioner. Dora's responsibilities did not end with her own children. She raised grandchildren, nieces and nephews. In a sense, she operated an "unlicensed" orphanage.[8]

She died at Cushing in 1954 at age eighty-two, an icon to her progeny.

ELLA HERMANN DOUTHITT
(1862-1942)
One in Thousands

The daughter of German emigrants, Ella Hermann Douthitt never did anything spectacular. She never did any "man work" for money. She did "woman work," as people in her days considered it. That covered the entire spectrum of labor required

Below: The daughter of German immigrants, Ella Hermann Douthitt had a most unusual background. A homesteader at Hennessey, she kept a diary of a sad life that became a happier one. (Courtesy Jeff and Reba Jennings)

to operate a home and care for a family.[9] In later years she did much of it alone. But Ella had an outlet and ambition enough to fill her loneliness. She kept a daily diary of life on the frontier.[10]

Born in Kansas City, Missouri, to J. and Mary Vincent Hermann, Ella was young when her family moved to the farm at Pittsburg, Kansas.[11] Her first language was German, which she learned from both parents. They told about their former experiences and how they had come to be in America.[12] Ella's father had lived on the verge of roguery. He had killed a man in Germany and, like Moses in Egypt, had fled. He went to Italy, was captured, and wound up a lieutenant in the Italian Army. From there he had come to New Orleans, Louisiana.[13]

The girl's mother possessed two pearl-handled pistols. She traded them to a boat captain for a ticket to New Orleans. An epidemic of smallpox was raging, so quarantines were in order. The two Germans boarded a northbound boat on the Mississippi River, where they met. With so much in common, it seemed destined they meet and come together in marriage. They became Ella's parents.[14]

When Ella made a little girlfriend in Kansas, she knew only one English word: "apple." The little girl became Ella's language teacher. What formal education she got was in a Catholic school. She was much older, she said, before she began thinking, as well as speaking, in English.[15]

In 1882, at age twenty, she married Edmond Page Douthitt in Pittsburg. By then Ella was well educated in "woman work" and was educating herself literally by reading everything she could lay her hands on and writing her diary.[16] Her husband, a native of Pennsylvania, was a mason and bricklayer. He had learned the trade from his father John. A follower of Alexander Campbell, John built churches, using his sons as laborers. On occasion, church members could not pay for the building, so John forgave the debts. This made life difficult for his family.[17]

Edmond became disillusioned with the practice and went his own way. He prospered in Kansas. He was near when the Unassigned Lands in Indian Territory opened for settlement in 1889. Edmond made the run and got 160 acres of land at Bison Spring near Hennessey south of present-day Enid.[18]

In that raw plains country, the Douthitts settled in a dugout, as many other runners did. Ella hated the treeless landscape, the dust and the heat. Besides, she was bearing children while her husband

Ella's sad life in a dugout terminated when she moved into this home in Hennessey and later to a duplicate of it in Sulphur. (Courtesy Jeff and Reba Jennings)

worked away from home much of the time. She directed her interest to things in the area and wrote about them.

The town of Hennessey, for instance, shot up overnight, and soon a post office was granted. It was named for Patrick Hennessee, a freighter on the old Chisholm Cattle Trail. Hennessee's two-wagon caravan, loaded with grain, had been en route to Fort Sill when Indians attacked it. They killed Hennessee and burned his wagons[19]. Ella hoped that such tragedies would never happen again. She wanted to leave. Edmond built a house in Hennessey and bought an interest in the Enid Pioneer Telephone Company. In 1890 the area became Oklahoma Territory. Things were looking better, but Ella still could not make friends with the plains.[20]

In 1905 the town of Sulphur in the Chickasaw Nation was experiencing its third birth. It was booming. Edmond and son Hermann got lots across the street from each other and decided to move on Edmond's. Then tragedy struck![21] One of the twins, Minnie, died from a ruptured appendix. That left Bernice, Cecil, and John. In mourning, the family elected to follow a different life.

Edmond brought the body of Minnie to Sulphur in one wagon, while John and a black driver brought the furniture in another. The rest of the family came on a train. John told about reaching the river at Purcell. It was in flood. The movers had to stop.[22] A sign forbade Negroes to remain there after dark. The driver quaked, but what could they do but wait? John went to sleep, but not for long. He awoke to the prayers of the black man, asking God to make the river go down. He got his wish, and they traveled on.

The Douthitt family buried their loved one in a cemetery northeast of town, then lived in a barn until the men could get a house built.[23] A duplicate of the one in Hennessey, this house was two stories of red brick with eight rooms. Its white gingerbread trim gave it a rare elegance. There were trees, and Ella loved them, but she set out more and planted flowers. She tended the cow and processed the milk, raised chickens, made a garden, and preserved much of its produce. She never failed to write regularly in her diary, including the kind of day it was.[24]

One could compose an historic almanac by Ella's weather reports: "Today, when a tornado came, I pushed the trunk of potatoes against the door....Today was hot and dry....This evening a blizzard struck....The day dawned on ice and snow...."[25]

Now old enough to support themselves, the children were of great concern to Ella. For a while both boys worked out of town with Edmond, then Herman centered on education. He earned his Ph.D. and became a professor of geology at the University of Kansas in Lawrence. Bernice attended a business school in Ada and worked for the telephone company. Cecil became a teacher in area schools.[26]

Ella wrote about their comings and goings. Cecil came often, the others seldom. "Surely," Ella wrote in her diary, "I'll get a card from Edmond (or John) tomorrow....I haven't got a letter from Hermann (or Edmond) in a week (or two weeks)...."

Ella wrote about the animals too. She "was sad when they had to put the cow away." She wrote

Below: This is one type of dugout used by settlers much like the ones used by the Biles and Douthitts. (Courtesy Harper County Historical Society)

about driving the horse and buggy to the country and about walking to town on various occasions. It was a happy message when someone came home.

A most intuitive person, Ella never ceased reading. She knew something about most everything. Many people consulted her for advice. Her home was always open for them, as well as for her family.[27]

Edmond died on a trip to Enid, while Ella died at the place she loved among the trees and flowers.[28] Ella represents the multitude of pioneer women who came, who saw and who helped develop the land called Oklahoma.

HARRIET PATRICK GILSTRAP
(1870-1970+)
Her Success Stalked by Failure

Harriet Patrick Gilstrap's first major success was winning a race for a homestead against the odds. It was during the second such run, which was into the Sac-Fox reservation on September 22, 1891. Her father, Colonel Lee Patrick, held her horse until all the other runners on that line dashed away.[29] Also one of the runners, a young man on a very fast horse had vowed to get the same 160-acre plot Harriet wanted. And he got a head start.[30]

The reason Colonel Patrick held Harriet's horse was the fact that he was Indian agent for the five tribes located on that reservation: Sac-Fox, Pottawatomie, Iowa, Shawnee, and Kickapoo, and he did not want anyone thinking he had given his daughter an advantage.[31]

When her horse was released, Harriet bounded away, dodging tree limbs, circumventing thickets, and jumping ditches. Her horse was in a lather when she reached her chosen plot. Off she bounded, stabbed her stake into the earth, and was rejoicing over her good fortune when the young man dashed up. His horse panted and blew steam from his nostrils. "I got lost," the young man said, dejectedly, but accepted his failure with grace.[32]

Harriet's work was only beginning. She had to improve the place and live there before she received a patent. Being a teacher at the Agency school, she had money for some construction. A laborer at the Agency built a storybook-type, one-room structure among the oaks. It looked more like a misplaced doll house than a pioneer's cabin on the frontier. Harriet moved in and had the 160 acres fenced.[33]

Her first venture into agribusiness was cattle. They soon died. She then invested in hogs, and they died. Discouraged, Harriet sold her homestead for

Harriet Patrick Gilstrap, teacher at the Sac and Fox Agency in 1891, made the land run and won—temporarily. (Courtesy Oklahoma Historical Society)

$3,000 and returned to the field of education.[34] This time she went to Haskell Institute in Kansas and later to the Quapaw Agency in northeast Indian Territory as principal. Her next move was back to the Sac-Fox Agency where her brother had become the agent.[35]

Another major success for Harriet was meeting Harry B. Gilstrap, editor of the *Chandler News* and secretary of the newly organized Oklahoma Press Association. The couple married in 1899 at the home of a relative in Illinois.[36] They returned to Chandler where Gilstrap held membership in the National Guard. When the United States entered World War I in 1917, Gilstrap went into service and rose to the rank of major.[37] By then the couple lived in Washington, D.C., and had three sons: Lee, Sam, and Harry, Jr. All of them grew up to become officers in the army—captain and lieutenants respectively.[38]

Four young pioneers in Indian regalia are engrossed in a game of cards. Second from right is Harriet Patrick Gilstrap, others unidentified. (Courtesy Oklahoma Historical Society)

The family returned to Oklahoma where Major Gilstrap became head of the Veteran's Administration. Harriet received the honor of "Deaconess of Life" in the Christian Church and devoted her spare time to serving in that capacity.[39]

She was born on a farm near Centropolis, Kansas, in 1870. Sometime after that event, Lee Patrick got an assignment as Indian Agent in the Territory. The family moved, stopping first at Oklahoma City. They bought supplies and headed for the Sac and Fox Agency, some fifty miles northeast. On today's map it would be five miles south of Stroud. Most of the way they had to make their own road, and it was rugged.[40]

The Agency, which had been established in 1869, served the Sac and Fox, Pottawatomie, Shawnee, Iowa, and Kickapoo tribesmen and was the center of a small settlement. It stood among sad-looking trees. The Indians had stripped off the bark and used it to build their lodges—wickiups and rough huts.[41] Besides the Agency, there was a boarding school, opened in 1872, a sawmill, and a post office in Chief Moses Keokuk's store. The United States government authorized the post office in 1875.

Harriet got a job as a postal clerk and recalled many of the interesting people and events surrounding it. The Daltons of gang infamy lived in the vicinity and frequented the establishment. She laughed about visiting and matching pennies with them.[42] She went from that job to teaching at Shawneetown Mission. Located south of the North Canadian River from present-day Shawnee, it was under the supervision of Patrick's agency. Harriet taught all grades at a salary of fifty dollars monthly—very good for that era.[43]

All, however, was not pleasant. Bedbugs were menacing. She sunned, aired, and treated her mattress with whatever was available—coal oil being one remedy—and tried to convince others to do likewise. Water also was a problem. Settlers hauled it in barrels, a very unsanitary method.[44] Harriet returned to the Agency to teach. The children were well dressed and had new names. Agent Patrick and his staff had given them such family names as those of presidents, vice presidents, and others of note or notion.[45]

At least two of Harriet's students were destined for fame—Jim Thorpe and Ernest Spybuck. Thorpe became the world's best-known athlete, while Spybuck excelled in art. He was self-taught. Thorpe's twin brother, Charley, was Harriet's student also, but he did not live long enough to become famous. He contracted typhoid during an epidemic and died in her arms.[46] "Charley was a good student," Harriet said, "but Jim was incorrigible." It was during this time at the Agency that Harriet dismissed school for a day and made her race for land.

She was living in Oklahoma City when she reached one hundred years of age. The exact date of her death is unavailable.[47]

MATTIE BEAL PAYNE
(1878-1931)
"Hello Girl" Snares Fame

Of more than 10,000 women who made the runs and lottery for land during the openings of Oklahoma Territory to non-Indians, Mattie Beal is the most remembered. A twenty-three-year-old telephone operator in Wichita, Kansas, Mattie read in a local 1901 paper about the forthcoming lottery for homesteads in the Kiowa, Comanche, Kiowa-Apache, and Wichita-Caddo reservations.[48] Registration was scheduled for July 10-26 of that year at El Reno and Fort Sill. The drawings would be held on July 29 and the opening itself on August 6. Mattie became interested.[49]

Against everybody's warning of danger, she decided to take a chance. In addition, she persuaded her friend and dressmaker, Florence Allen, to go along.[50] The girls boarded a train from Wichita

21

One of 164,000 who registered for the land drawing in 1901, Mattie Beal Payne was most fortunate. She is shown here with her husband, Charles Payne. (Courtesy Hugh Corwin and Prairie Lore*)*

registered at El Reno and 29,000 at Fort Sill. El Reno chalked up 10,000 women registrants. No record was found of the number who registered at Fort Sill or those who made the runs.

While strolling in a Wichita park one day, Mattie found a horseshoe. "I hope it's a sign of good luck," she said and took it home. Shortly thereafter, she was walking home from work when a man stepped in front of her and snapped a picture.

"What are you doing!" she exclaimed.

"Haven't you heard?" he asked. "You have just won homestead number two in the Oklahoma Territory lottery. It's all over the wires. I'm from the newspaper and I want your picture with the story."[52] It took a few moments for Mattie to believe the man and regain her composure. He told her that the drawing had been held in El Reno, where all the sealed bids had been assembled.

This was only the beginning of much publicity for the young telephone operator. Florence Allen also got land, but her name was so far down the list that by the time she learned of her success, the sensation of winning had worn off.[53]

The first winner of a homestead had been James T. Woods, a hardware clerk in Weatherford, Oklahoma Territory. The good fortune of young and beautiful Mattie overshadowed him. So did his avarice.[54] Mattie Beal's picture and story appeared

Below: Charles and Mattie Beal Payne's home in Lawton is now owned by the Lawton Heritage Association and is open for visitors. It is listed in the National Register of Historic Places. (From the author's collection)

to El Reno. On their arrival, they were engulfed by throngs of people. They learned that these people were from all over the United States and some foreign countries. Fortunately, they met a newspaper man who helped them find a room for the night. It cost two dollars.[51]

The next day, there was a special table for women to register set up in the government building. The crowd was so pressing, the two young women could not reach it. Then chivalry rose to resolve their predicament. "Give the ladies a chance!" someone shouted. Soldiers on duty went to Mattie and Florence and led them to the desk. They registered, but the crowd kept swelling. The girls decided that they had no chance to win, so they returned home and to work.

Newspaper stories further darkened their hopes of winning. The papers stated that 135,000 had in papers all over the country. Her wealth was estimated from $20,000 to $40,000. In those days, that sum was enough to open a bank. Hundreds of letters poured in to her, many containing proposals of marriage. She never answered them, but romance lay in her path.[55]

Before the day to choose homesteads, Mattie and her brother Frank, a railroad conductor, went to the Fort Sill-Lawton area. They got as far as Marlow on the train, then hired a spring wagon to take them the rest of the way. Also in the wagon were Mr. and Mrs. Joe White. He had been appointed the new postmaster at Lawton.[56] The foursome arrived in Lawton to find it consisted of a couple of frame buildings, a prairie full of dust and tents, and 25,000 people milling among hawkers for various kinds of business. There were gambling dens, hotels, drug stores, restaurants, entertainers, and a hundred saloons—all in tents.[57] One of the entertainers was the "Mud Eater." Surprisingly, there was plenty of food, but it was "garnished with dust and flies."

James Woods had chosen the only available land joining the townsite. It was a strip a quarter of a mile wide on the south. Resentful homesteaders branded him "Hog Woods." Mattie chose the next land south. It was on a hill overlooking the townsite and in view of the Wichita Mountains to the northwest.[58]

The Kansan went home a short time, then returned to Lawton to establish a home. By then Charles Payne from Fulton, New York, had bought an interest in a lumber yard there. It was a natural setup for Mattie to meet him.[59] She met another man from New York. He bought a buggy and a team of spotted horses, then built a shed near Mattie's two-room house. "Use the buggy and horses any time," he told Mattie and her brother. Soon he appeared as driver. Mattie avoided his attention until he gave up and returned to New York.

Charles Payne entranced her. They entered into a courtship and within a few months became engaged. They were married in the home of Mattie's mother in Wichita.[60]

In 1902 Lawton had a population of 8,000, but many remaining campers needed land. City officials prevailed upon the Paynes to divide their land into lots and hold an auction. After much consideration, they agreed. Lawyers got permission from Washington, D.C., for the division. The Paynes set aside land for a park, a Presbyterian church, and Lincoln School, but retained some for family use. The auction began on July 25, 1902. At its completion, a thousand more residents needed homes. The Paynes made little on the auction, but Charles' business flourished. The Mattie Beal addition was soon incorporated into Lawton.[61]

The couple built a new home of neoclassic Greek architecture at a cost of $30,000. That was an enormous amount in those days. Finished in 1908, it became Lawton's place for social gatherings. The couple had three daughters: LaHoma, Louise, and Martha Helen. They studied music locally and at the University of Oklahoma. Mattie died in 1931 following an appendectomy. Survivors sold the family home. It changed hands several times; one of the operators divided it into apartments. It began to deteriorate. Charles died in 1947.[62]

The Lawton Heritage Association raised money to purchase and restore this beloved old haven and got it listed on the National Register of Historic Homes. Now returned to its original grandeur, the mansion stands as a monument to a "Hello Girl" (telephone operator) and to an exciting era of this state's development.[63] It is the site of Heritage meetings and is open to the public for visiting on designated days.

* * * * * * * * * * * *

Who were the women in Indian Territory and what were they doing when the homesteaders arrived? Except for the wealthy, who could afford servants, they were homemaking and raising families. For the Indians, that included everything from constructing the tepees to teaching their daughters how to pound corn into meal. As wives, teachers and missionaries, white women concentrated on serving others and surviving. All races endured much drudgery, but considered it a way of life, as the lives of the following women will illustrate.

Chapter 2
HOMEMAKERS

SIPPIA PAUL HULL
(1843-after 1929)
Child of the Wilderness

Named for her Chickasaw mother and her mother's native state, Mississippi, Sippia Paul Hull was born in the pristine wilderness of Cross Timbers in the Chickasaw Nation. At that time deer, antelope, and buffalo grazed in multitudes among villages of friendly Indians and camps of wild ones.[1] The wild ones depredated the friendly tribesmen and the few, scattered whites in the region. They robbed, burned shelters, and sometimes killed anyone they considered to be an interloper. They scalped one of Sippia's friends, a young man named Courtney. As a result, the settlers, especially the women, lived in constant fear.[2]

In 1851 the United States government established Fort Arbuckle a short distance from Sippia's home and appointed her father, Smith Paul, a white man, as agent to the friendly Indians. He was a wealthy man with slaves to farm many acres of land. He became the supplier of agricultural products to the fort.[3]

In 1929 Sippia wrote many stories about her youth and left them on file in the archives of the Pauls Valley Memorial Library. She remembered the flight of the Union Army at the beginning of the Civil War (1861) and the coming of the Confederates. She told of hiding in the cornfield and woods during raids by the wild tribes and the arrow-filled horses they left behind.[4] But that era had a good side. At night, while her mother worked and told Indian legends, Sippia learned how to manufacture material. She heated cotton to help free the lint they had to pull from the seeds. She spun the lint into thread and wove it into enough cloth to make herself a dress.[5] A man with a miniature gin wandered into the community and removed seed from lint mechanically. While trying to learn to operate the contraption, one of Sippia's brothers broke it.

Mrs. Paul taught her to make summer hats for the boys with wheat straw and winter caps from coonskins. Smith Paul made shoes from cowhides. Sippia did not like the shoes, but there was no way to get any better kind.[6] At hog killing time, the girl helped make sausage by pounding the meat in a mortar with a pestle. They had no sausage mills.

After the War, settlers heard that the Cheyennes were threatening a raid. Colonel George Custer, who had been stationed at Fort Arbuckle at the time, got orders to march against the Indians. He and his troops left from Camp Supply, farther north. Among those who joined him were Sippia's brothers.[7] They headed for Chief Black Kettle's camp on the Washita River and returned to celebrate. They held a scalp dance, which lasted three weeks and drew people from as far away as Texas. "I remember," Sippia wrote, "the scalps they brought home and Black Kettle's coat. The wife of a friendly Indian chief wore it."[8] Although Sippia left no report of the battle, history gives a gruesome account of Custer's attack and massacre of the Cheyennes at that time.

Smith Paul hired teachers to come live with the family and teach the children. He hired ministers also and provided a meeting place. Because the area was so far from civilization, neither teachers nor ministers stayed very long.[9]

At age sixteen, Sippia married a Texan, Jim Arnold, and bore a daughter Tamsie. One account said that Paul outfitted Arnold with a wagon and team for a trip to Texas after supplies. Arnold left, and the Pauls never heard from him again.[10] Sippia was said to have considered Arnold dead and decided she needed more formal education. By then, Fort Arbuckle had been abandoned, and Fort Sill was active. The Quakers had established the Kiowa Indian School there, so Sippia took her daughter and went to enroll.[11]

Fortunately for her, she secured board, room, and care for Tamsie from Tomassa Chandler, a Mexican woman, whose unusual story is told elsewhere in this book. Also Sippia met an Englishman, William Hull, and became attracted to him. Hull worked for the government under Indian Agent Lawrie Tatum. When Sippia left the school, Hull followed and became a blacksmith in the Paul community. This was on the stage and freight route to Fort Sill, so Hull prospered.[12]

He and Sippia married. He built a commodious home beside the Washita River near Whitebead and

Holding her birthday cake, Bessie Dink Edwards Chapman poses with her young descendants, who adored her. (Courtesy Patti Russell)

help she needed," Patti said, "was for someone to tell her when the water was boiling. She canned boxes and boxes of food and shared it with everyone who came to visit." In 1953 the Chapmans' daughter Virginia returned home with three children: Patti, a baby, her brother, and sister. Virginia worked away from home while "Granny became a mother to us," Patti said. "By then, all Granny could see was images of people. The light hurt her eyes, so she protected them with a bonnet. It became her trademark."[51]

Grandpa Hank died. Virginia remarried, and the other children scattered near and far to establish their own homes. Patti continued living with Granny. She assisted and observed her in every way. Weekdays, Granny got up before dawn, cooked her breakfast, washed her clothes by hand, and hung them on the line. Sundays and Wednesday evenings she and whoever else was there attended services at the Assembly of God Church. Granny tithed from her "fixed income." She visited the sick and prepared food for anyone in need.[52] She kept children, entertained them with stories, and telephoned anyone she heard was ill or in trouble.

Granny's method of writing was unique. Patti said, "She would roll the paper completely around one pencil, unroll it once, write a line with another pencil, and continue the process until she finished the page. The only thing she couldn't do was dot the i's and cross the t's.

"Granny could quilt, too," Patti continued, "after someone threaded her needle. Through the medium of touch, her stitches and lines were perfect. Her method of washing dishing was similar. To insure cleanliness, she rubbed her fingers across every item before rinsing it."

Patti and other nearby family members took Granny to quilting bees, shopping, visiting the sick, and to the cemetery to commune with Hank. Young members of the family always took their friends to meet her. "She was such an inspiration and entertainer," Patti said. "They left lighthearted and laughing at her quips and stories."

After Patti married, had a child, and moved away, Granny chose to live in a nursing home. "She didn't want to be a burden to her children," was said to be the reason. But she kept busy. She asked the nurses to let her do such chores as folding the laundry. When family members took her for a drive, Granny amused them with stories about the people in the home.[53] Before her life ebbed away in 1980, Granny asked to go to the funeral home. There she made her funeral arrangements. She chose the casket, the scripture reading, and songs. Again, "She didn't want to be a burden to her children."

Those of the four generations remaining, plus many friends, still have problems "doing without Granny." They ease their loneliness by writing and telling her story.[54] Granny operated an "orphanage and a refuge" as well as a home.

****

Records of women in agriculture have appeared since the story of Ruth in the Bible about 1300 B.C. or before. Such work for them continued through the centuries. After the American Civil War many widows brought their children to Indian Territory to farm and raise livestock. The profession of agriculturist continues to this day.

Chapter 3
AGRICULTURISTS

RHODA PITCHLYNN HOWELL
(1814-1911)
A Choctaw Widow of Renown

Even though the year was 1866 and the place was near the fading Fort Arbuckle in the Chickasaw Nation, Rhoda Pitchlyn Howell was said to know something about everything.[1] Many people came great distances to her for information and advice. In reality, Rhoda, whose Indian name was *Pashuma*, meaning "red haired woman," was a counselor, a psychologist, and a physician, but one without credentials, credit, or fee. She would not accept payment, but people showered her with gifts. Even cattle.

But why would not Rhoda be wise and full of knowledge? The mother of fourteen children, she had learned from experience to feed, clothe, and protect her young and to teach them survival, both physical and mental. In addition, Rhoda had learned from her forebears.[2]

Her parents, John and Sophia Folsom Pitchlynn, were Choctaw leaders east of the Mississippi River when she was born on July 1, 1814, in the vicinity of Columbus. She had a brother, Chief Peter Pitchlynn, who was devoted to education and the welfare of the tribe and who served as its representative in Washington. He was also involved in the Civil War.[3]

Rhoda married Calvin Howell, who was of Scotch-Irish extraction. He was said to be a doctor before the family came west. Some of their children were born in Mississippi, and at least one of them, Thomas P. Howell, attended school in Tennessee. He received a medical degree in Maryland.[4] The Calvin Howells came to Indian Territory in the 1830s and settled at Eagletown near the border of Arkansas. The site was famous for the many eagles which nested on the banks of the nearby Mountain Fork River.[5]

Soon after their arrival, Calvin Howell set up a cotton gin, and the family helped develop the community from a wilderness. Several of the settlers brought slaves who contributed immensely until after the Civil War. Eagletown grew to have stores, hotels, churches, blacksmith shops, and mills. Roads and ferries across the streams led to farms and plantations. Colonel David Folsom operated a salt work, which produced twenty bushels a day.[6] Cyrus and Mrs. Byington came as missionaries and established Stockbridge in the 1830s. It was there that Byington compiled the *Dictionary of the Choctaw Language*. Within a short time, there were twelve mission schools in the Choctaw Nation, and the number continued to increase.[7] These schools taught not only the three Rs, but also skills for farming and homemaking. Stockbridge, for instance, had thirteen looms and, in a short time, women were producing thousands of yards of material.

The tribe had a government which had problems with whites promoting whiskey. The Choctaw Lighthorsemen (police) confiscated whiskey handled by their own people, tied the handlers to a

Below: Left a widow with fourteen children in 1866, Rhoda Pitchlynn Howell, a Choctaw, moved from Eagletown, Indian Territory, to fading Fort Arbuckle and operated a ranch. Her family became prominent in agriculture, banking, and other professions. (Courtesy Photographics, Davis)

tree, and scourged them. They executed habitual lawbreakers.[8]

Although there was a drought, a plague of cholera, and other problems from 1833 to 1861, the era was considered the Choctaw's "Golden Age". Then came the Civil War (1861-65) and decline. Schools closed and Confederate troops took over the buildings, as well as the forts. Business and industry were curtailed. Battles and depradation by the wild tribes racked Indian Territory.[9]

Rhoda Pitchlynn Howell suffered through it all, while still bearing children. Then, a year after the war ended, she lost her husband Calvin and a son. As is the case with most everyone, those deaths marked a turning point in Rhoda's life.[10] She moved her remaining family into the Chickasaw Nation near Fort Arbuckle. Located on the north side of the Arbuckle Mountains, the fort was still in operation and of some protection. She became a farmer-rancher.[11] The Howell children included Thomas, Fannie, John, Ellen, Margaret, Calvin, Arabella, Mary, Joseph, Ed, Isabella, Peter, William, and Roena.

Isabella died, and as was customary Rhoda chose a site on the family farm for burial.[12] That site started the Howell Cemetery, today located at the northeast corner of the intersection of state Highway 7 and Interstate 35 in Murray County.[13]

In 1875, Thomas P. Howell came to settle near his mother and siblings and practice medicine. He engaged in farming and ranching. By then Fort Arbuckle had "given birth" to Fort Sill, and the fort's sutler, Tom Grant, had bought the remains for twenty-seven cents an acre. He also was in the farm-ranch business.[14] Doctor Howell married Lizzie Grant, daughter of Tom and Mary J. Love Grant, then built a spacious three-story mansion in the rich valley of the Washita River.[15]

Of course, Rhoda Pitchlynn Howell was involved. With several more children, she was further involved with weddings, especially with the girls. And there was the Howell Church, otherwise known as Oak Ridge, for convenience. It was of the Methodist faith. Fannie married an employee of the family ranch, Nick Butterly. He had come from Ireland a few years before. They established a large ranch in the Arbuckle Mountains and, although he died in 1903, some of the sections of land still carry his name (1992).

Ellen Louise married Matt Wolf, a Texan. He was said to have fenced ten thousand acres for ranching and built a two-room log house with a dogtrot (breezeway) between. Each room had a fireplace. Besides ranching, Wolf also established the village of Washita on his premises. A post office and store lasted from 1887 to 1900, when the residents moved to Davis. Margaret Howell married Thomas Grant, after his first wife died, and the family continued to live at the old fort. Arabella married a man named Wright, and Mary married one named Camp. The names of the others' companions are not available, but from all indications, Rhoda P. Howell's children were credits to her and to the area they helped develop.[16]

When there were no school buildings, they provided space in their homes for classrooms and hired governesses to live in and teach, not only their own children but also those of their neighbors. The Howells were some of the first bankers in the area, where several of their descendants still live.

At about eighty-two years of age, Rhoda Pitchlynn Howell lost her eyesight but maintained her otherwise good health. She also kept her sense of humor and continued to advise anyone who came to seek her help.[17] At age ninety-seven she took pneumonia and died. That was in 1911. The great but quiet lady is buried in the well-kept family cemetery among many of her descendants and their companions.[18]

JIMY EARLENE BRADY ROSE
(1929 -   )
A Rancher, an Equestrienne, and Much More

Jimy Earlene Brady Rose could wear many logos: "The Answer to a Prayer.... She Carried a Brand.... Branded EJ.... Her Grandfather's Son.... Her Gift: a Portion of Self" and many more.[19] The owner and operator of three ranches in Carter County, South Central Oklahoma, Jimy and her husband Eldridge Ed Rose live on the one which lies along Caddo Creek south of Springer. While he takes care of his business in oil, Jimy oversees the ranches. Not only that, but she participates in[20] numerous cultural, religious and educational projects in her community and in nearby Ardmore.

Although Jimy has two full-time and one part-time employees, she rides the range in a pickup as a regular hand. Her work day begins at 5:00 a.m., and by 6:30 she is on the road to one of her pastures.[21] Her job depends on the season of the year. It changes from fencing pastures into paddocks,

As one of the "Glamour Western Ranch Girls" at Madison Square Gardens in New York City, Jimy Brady Rose and a friend led a parade down Fifth Avenue a few years ago. Jimy operates three ranches in the Ardmore area. (Courtesy Jimy Brady Rose)

planting wheat, cutting hay, and graveling roads to tagging animals, changing them from one paddock to another, to hunting for fence-jumpers and caring for newborn calves. Sometimes there is a sick animal to treat or a dead one to bury.[22]

When Jimy is at home, the telephone or doorbell rings every few minutes during the day and often into the night. But that is the normal life of a rancher. When Jimy took over the family property in 1971, "not by choice," her father had been deceased two years. Her mother, who was ill, was living with her. (Her mother died two years later.)[23] Due to those circumstances, the original ranch had deteriorated. Its future was dark and so was Jimy's. Fate had made it so. "A tornado had flattened seven barns and torn up the ranch" in general. Representatives of the Internal Revenue Service were at her door. "They demanded figures," Jimy said, "I could not comprehend in value."[24]

"How could I, a single woman, run a ranch and make enough to pay the IRS, rebuild the barns and reclaim the soil, fertilize the grass, and rebuild the herd of cattle? The fences, also, needed repairs. I had to depend on my early training," Jimy continued, "and God."[25]

The results were three highly qualified employ-ees: Ray O. Dyer, his son Jim Dyer, and Ike McGee. "Ray had retired from the Agricultural Division of Noble Foundation," Jimy said, "but he died soon after I employed him. His son Jim Dyer, former editor of *Progressive Farmer*, continued what his father had started and became manager. Jim had a master's degree in Agricultural Journalism from Oklahoma State University."[26] Jimy and Ray centered their efforts on building an outstanding herd of Brangus cattle, while McGee continued his long service at the ranch. He helped in numerous ways. To her Grandfather Eave's brand of "JE" Jimy added a bar, thus personalizing it, "*JE*" for Jimy Earlene. Within four years, the ranch reached its promotional slogan, "Tomorrow's Beef Today."[27]

Jimy was so interwoven with her ancestors and the ranch, her story could not be told without a glimpse of them. Her maternal grandparents and mother—James (Jim) Jackson, Edna Earl Payne and Mamie Aslee Eaves—left the now famous Texas community of Lonesome Dove in 1892. Traveling in three covered, ox-drawn wagons, they plodded north up to the Indian Territory settlement of Elk, later called Pooleville, and said, "This is it."[28] There they rented forty acres from the Chickasaws and lived in the wagons until they got a cabin built. They worked hard in that raw land and prospered.[29]

When Jim Eaves made the thirty-eight miles southeast to Ardmore, he brought back supplies for his neighbors as well as for his own family. Among those neighbors was a couple named "Brown." They seemed as friendly and ordinary as all the rest. In 1894, however, they shocked the entire Territory and far beyond. Trailed to Elk by United States marshals, Mr. Brown was killed, and Mrs. Brown, while returning from Ardmore, was taken into custody. The couple proved to be Mr. and Mrs. Bill Dalton. He and a companion had recently robbed a bank in Longview, Texas.[30] Mrs. Dalton took her husband's body to her former home in California for burial.

When restrictions were removed from Indian land, Eaves bought a few acres. He raised cattle, sheep, and farm crops: grain, hay, alfalfa. And there were always horses. In time he owned twenty-seven sections of land skirting the Arbuckle Mountains. He built a new home in Pooleville and one in Ardmore.[31] The latter one was of Valentine-card beauty. Mrs. Eaves and Mamie stayed in it so Mamie could attend high school. She had finished elementary school in Pooleville.[32] From high school,

Mamie went to Hargrove College and the College of Industrial Arts at Denton, Texas. She earned a teacher's certificate; then romance entered her life. She married James Ray Brady in 1911.[33]

After the couple had an extended honeymoon in Mexico, Mamie taught school at Pooleville, Buttermilk, and Round-Up. In addition, she taught piano and violin at Pooleville and in Ardmore.[34] A devout Baptist, Mamie worked in the church and assisted in raising funds for at least sixteen congregations at one time. She helped the young preachers also.[35]

"Mother was the most real Christian and the hardest working woman," Jimy wrote in the family history, "I've ever known.... Her heart was as big as the whole out-of-doors...and I shall always remember her beautiful rose garden...."

Jimy's father James, "J" Ray Brady, was another Texan. In 1887 he came with his father on the first train into Ardmore. They brought a load of flour from their mill at Gainesville. They liked Indian Territory so well they moved there two years later and went into business.[36] Young Brady worked in the store and attended school. He graduated from Hargrove College and Selvidge Business College before going into business for himself. Besides operating a grocery store, he managed an opera house and farmed. Later he had a skating rink and was an expert on wheels.[37]

As if that were not enough, Brady bought and sold land, always reserving the royalty. He and his wife lost a baby in about 1914, and the doctor said they would never have another. Determined to prove him wrong, they hoped and prayed for another child.[38] The 1920s were prosperous years. Like spring, oil was "bustin' out all over" Oklahoma. People were taking chances in every direction. Eaves took one when he signed a friend's note for $80,000, mortgaging his ranches and cattle. The "friend," who was to go into the oil business, changed the figures to $180,000.[39] When his business failed, the bank took Eaves' property, leaving him a horse on which to ride away and start again. It so happened, Eaves had given his daughter Mamie her separate estate in 1922. It was the family's original homesite. That was a blessing for the entire group.

Another blessing fell on the family in 1929. J. Ray and Mamie Brady's prayers were answered with the birth of a daughter. They named her "Jimy" for all the Jameses in the family.[40] Growing up with four adults between the ranch and the city of Ardmore, Jimy became saturated in culture and religion on one hand and ranches and animals on the other. She rode a horse before she was a year old and owned one by the age of three. When she was five, her grandfather Eaves, who had emerged from bankruptcy, gave her a Shetland pony. She kept it in the back yard at the Brady home in Ardmore and rode it frequently.[41]

During the same time, Jimy learned thrift. She helped her grandfather on the ranch, and he gave her fifty cents. "A nickel of that is for the Lord," he told her, "a dime is for saving. The rest you can spend."[42] Jimy's mother was teaching her music and all the graces necessary to become a lady.

Both parents took her to rodeos where she won barrel races in Texas, Oklahoma, Kansas, and Arkansas. She became an accomplished horsewoman. And she became a property owner. Grandfather Eaves, who continued to prosper, gave Jimy a heifer calf to start a herd and 360 acres of pasture. She sold the land and bought a home in Ardmore and forty acres along Caddo Creek north of Ardmore. It joined her parents' land.[43] All through high school, Jimy participated in a multitude of activities, especially music and drama. Her equestrienne activities paid off in honors. She won six titles as queen. "Several times she was one of the Glamour Western Ranch Girls at Madison Square Gardens, New York City and at Boston Garden Rodeos. She and a friend led a parade on horseback down Fifth Avenue."[44] After high school, Jimy attended Monticello College, a girls' finishing school at Godfrey, Illinois.

Below: Jimy Brady Rose's daughters Glena and Linda Wood were in parades early in life. Here Glena leads their Shetland pony while Linda rides in the miniature covered wagon built by their grandfather, Roy Brady. (Courtesy Jimy Brady Rose)

In 1950 she married Glen Wood. He became a rodeo announcer, and they followed the rodeo circuit. They had two daughters, Glena and Linda. When the girls were old enough, they participated in rodeo activities.[45] For a while, Glena and Linda led fairy tale lives. Their Grandfather Brady built a miniature covered wagon for them. They became the chief attraction in parades. The grandfather rode in the replica of a Concord stage he had previously built. Both vehicles were pulled by Shetland ponies. So were the rubber-tired cart and Roman chariot Brady constructed.[46]

But life had its midnights. The girls' parents divorced. Heavy hearted, Jimy turned to her heritage and the scriptures and brought the situation into daylight. She got a job in a shop in Ardmore. Later she became an attendance clerk at Ardmore High School. In time she realized that her father and grandfather had trained her to manage a ranch, so she returned to country life.[47] She continued with the "JE" brand (they were joined at the back for her grandfather Jim Eaves, but added a bar, making it "*JE*").

Jimy succeeded. She supported her daughters, sending them through college and into life-sustaining professions before marriage. She restored her grandparents' original cabin on the ranch, opened it to the public as a museum in 1977, and got it placed on the National Register of Historic Places. That coincided with her grandfather's induction into the National Cowboys' Hall of Fame in Oklahoma City.[48]

The lady accumulated the three ranches, married Eldridge Ed Rose, then took on a new challenge. She became a compelling force in the Carter County Historical Society's establishment of a museum. It has become an outstanding institution in South Central Oklahoma.[49] Jimy's civic and humanitarian contributions had grown to such magnitude that by 1991 she became the subject of a "roast" at Ardmore to benefit the March of Dimes.[50] Jimy's most recent honor was the presentation of the Oklahoma Heritage Association's Award for History in 1992. It was in recognition of her contributions to the Carter County Historical Society and the newly established museum in Ardmore.[51]

To do the lady rancher justice, it would take a book larger than all the literary work she produced during those years: book reviews, a newspaper column and the family history, *What God Hath Blessed*. She wrote this history at the insistence of Dot Adkins, an employee of the *Daily Ardmoreite*. Dot compiled and edited the material, highlighting the qualities which inspired the suitable logos for Jimy.

MARY ANN JAMES
A Bison Rancher

Oklahoma women have always been involved in agribusiness as cattle and horse ranchers and farmers, but there is one who dared to raise the shaggy bison in mass. She is Mary Ann James of near Adair in the northeast section of the state.[52] Adair, a history maker within itself, is a town of 685 inhabitants (1990 census) in Mayes County between Tulsa and Miami. Its geography is good for such a venture.[53]

About 1983 Mary Ann entered bison ranching at Windsong Ranch. She grazes some 450 animals on two sections of land. Having to supplement their food only in winter and during drought, she considers bison easy to raise.[54] One of the most interesting characteristics Mary Ann observes about her herd is that all bison mothers calve about the same time—early spring. She and her employees can tell when the animals are ready to give birth. They begin moving to the highest point on the ranch, tagged "Buffalo Hill."[55] They not only go there to bear their young but, like the proverbial elephant, to die as well.

Mary Ann chose this unusual business because of the animals' dietary benefits. The meat has low fat and low cholesterol content. Would she recommend the business to others?[56] "It has been reward-

Below: Braving animals such as these, Mary Ann James operates the Windsong Bison Ranch in northeastern Oklahoma. (From the author's collection)

ing to me," she said, "and I suppose I'll stay with it for some time to come. It's getting harder to retire."

****

Throughout history, captives were often used in agriculture and other endeavors. The spoils of war since war began, captives were taken by Bible characters and men in general. In the Bible, Jacob's sons killed the men of Shechem and took their wives, children and animals. Black slaves in America were captives. So were hundreds of other people. The Indians took their share of captives. How four of them survived captivity is told in the following chapter.

Chapter 4
CAPTIVES

FRANCISCA MEDRANO
(1831-1931)
Runaway Slave Finds Success

Francisca Medrano, a Comanche captive, had faced hunger, torture, and the loss of babies, but she feared most to face a camera. "I'm asking Jesus," she said, "to let me live to be a hundred. If I let you put my picture on paper, I would die soon."[1] Francisca was talking to the Reverend A.E. Butterfield, a missionary, when she was ninety-seven years old. She lived near the Little Washita River between Fletcher and Union City, Oklahoma.[2]

The Comanches had taken Francisca in New Mexico Territory when she was about four years old (1835). According to one version of the event, the Indians also took her brother and sister. The three were divided among the raiders, and Francisca never saw the others again. Her captors traveled hours and hours, stopping only to eat and rest. They offered her some of their raw meat, but she refused to eat. Finally, hunger drove her to take a piece of burned horse flesh. She ate so ravishingly the Indians laughed and seemed pleased.[3]

At their camp, they made her a slave. She carried wood and water, cleaned hides, and tended ponies. But she could not do enough to satisfy them. They called her "Mexican" and beat her hands until they were deformed. Remembering her family and former home, she always said she was Aztec Indian.[4]

At an early age, she was sold or traded to a Kiowa warrior for a wife. She bore three babies, all of whom died. The Kiowa either died or was killed, and that tribe sold her back to a Comanche. He also mistreated her. She had a daughter, whom she named Marguerite, and the two of them escaped.[5] Francisca had heard that the United States Army would protect runaways, so she took her daughter and fled in the direction of Fort Sill. The wife of a Mexican freighter found them starving in a plum thicket. She took them to her home where they stayed a long time.

A freighter boarding in that home, Abilene Medrano, was another runaway. At age fifteen he had fled his home in Spain to avoid serving in the army when he reached age sixteen. He and Francisca became interested in each other. When the Comanches learned her whereabouts, they went to the commanding officer at Fort Sill and demanded her return. However, Abilene intervened in her behalf, so the Army refused to return her to the Indians.[6]

Francisca and Abilene married. They had three children: Louise, John (Juan), called "Pio," and Benifacio, called "Bonnie." Abilene was good to his family. At allotment time, he was one of a few non-Indians given a homestead and, no doubt, the only one who refused it. He reasoned that Indians should be the only ones to get land. Francisca accepted her allotment. It was located four miles northeast of Fletcher, the place they already occupied. The family prospered in horses and cattle.[7]

Louise married United States Marshal Frank Farwells. Pio went to work at Hollis and wrote his fiancée to join him and get married. When she arrived, he was not there, and no one ever heard of him again. That incident troubled Francisca the rest of her life. Bonnie became the "rock" of the family. He even preached his father's funeral.[8]

In 1893, Abilene and a friend named Mikecoby hauled lumber to build a small Methodist church in the vicinity of Union City (Canadian County) near the Little Washita River. He and Francisca became Protestants; however, she still occasionally made the sign of the cross.[9] This led people to believe she was still remembering a bit of her early childhood in a Catholic setting in New Mexico. She was active in the little church the rest of her life.

Sometime after age ninety-seven, Francisca agreed to pose for a picture if the Reverend Butterfield would stand beside her. He did, but the picture was destroyed in a fire.[10]

On Easter Sunday, 1931, members of the Little Washita congregation met to celebrate Francisca's one hundredth birthday and testify. The beloved and honored guest gave her testimony, sat down, and died. She had been granted one request: to live a hundred years.

peace and their trip to Fort Arbuckle, the troops planned their strategy. They had received orders to "punish" the Comanches for recent raids into Texas. Major Earl Van Dorn, leader of the cavalry, ordered nineteen-year-old Lieutenant Sul Ross to release the Indians' five hundred horses grazing nearby, then attack the south end of the village with 135 friendly Indians—Waco, Tawakoni, Tonkawa, and Caddo from the Brazos River reservation. Van Dorn would attack the north end.

After the horses were released, rifles and shotguns began spitting fire and lead, hatchets and knives flashed, and arrows whizzed. A group of Indians fled toward the creek. Ross, a Lieutenant Van Camp, a soldier named Alexander, and a Caddo Indian ran to intercept them, discovering that they were women and children.[25] When a second group dashed past, Ross recognized a girl about eight years old as white. He ordered the Caddo to grab her. She screamed, bit, scratched, and fought like a "wildcat," but the Caddo clung to her.

Some twenty-five Comanches cut off Ross from communications with Major Van Dorn on the north, shot Lieutenant Van Camp through the heart, then killed Alexander. One named Mohee, whom Ross had known at the reservation in Texas, grabbed Alexander's rifle and shot Ross, paralyzing him on one side.

The Indian snatched a butcher knife to scalp his victim, but a Comanche shouted a command, diverting his attention. Lieutenant James Majors, later a Confederate general, killed Mohee. Major Van Dorn caught an arrow in his shoulder and fell.[26] The Caddo and the protesting white child remained unharmed, probably because the Indians were afraid of killing her.

When the smoke and fog cleared about two hours later, five whites lay dead and seven wounded. Eighty or more Comanches and some Wichitas had been killed, many wounded, and several captured. Buffalo Hump and other Comanches escaped.[27] The troops burned the lodges and took all the horses and equipment, but the wounded officers tarried five or six days to recuperate. When Lieutenant Ross was able, his Indian troops put him on a litter between two mules and took him to Camp Radziminski, which had previously been established near present-day Tipton. Occasionally the Indians carried Ross while transporting the child—much against her will.[28]

At Camp Radziminski, Ross' group secured an

A Wichita village, near the current Rush Springs, Oklahoma, was the battleground where Lizzie Ross was rescued from the Comanches. (Courtesy Hugh Corwin)

"ambulance" to take him and the child to his family home at Waco, Texas. There she was thrust into strange surroundings and unable to communicate. Like Cinderella, her origin was never known. She had been with the Comanches since she could remember and therefore saw herself as red. To her, she belonged in a tepee or grass hut when she was not following the buffalo for food, clothing, and shelter.

Now, she was the "captive" of an illustrious white family of Texas Rangers, Indian fighters, and belles of Waco. She was confined in a new colonial house on an eighty-acre farm at the southwest corner of the town where slaves helped with the work.[29] Mrs. Katherine Ross, tagged "Mother of Waco," welcomed the little waif. So did Captain Shapley P. Ross, an Indian agent on the Brazos River reservation, and their eight children.[30]

The two older girls, Margaret (Mrs. W. M. Harris) and Mary (Mrs. George Barnard) had been married in a double ceremony in 1850 and had homes of their own. Peter, twenty-two, had recently returned from two years military training in New York. He now served as a captain in the Rangers by the authority of governor Sam Houston.[31] There was Annie, whose age was undetermined; Lieutenant Sul; Kate, twelve years old; Robert, ten; and William H., about four. Mervin died early in life.

Captain Shapley, who had helped establish Waco on the site of a former Waco Indian village, had built the first hotel in the town and served as its first postmaster. He also had built and operated a ferry across the Brazos River. It remained a thoroughfare to the west until a suspension bridge was built in 1870. This first-class family of the frontier "made a pet of the new child," finally taming her. Sul christened her "Lizzie" in honor of his fiancée, Miss Lizzie Tinsley, daughter of Doctor and Mrs. Tinsley of Waco. Little Lizzie had a creek upon which to play and children from whom to learn.[32]

When Lieutenant Sul recovered sufficiently, he returned to Wesleyan University at Florence, Alabama, where he graduated in 1859. Meanwhile, Mrs. Katherine was practicing her skills as a mother-teacher on Lizzie. She had taught the older children before private or public schools were available. Though no record can be found of Lizzie's formal education, it is believed that she attended Waco Female Academy. The school burned, thus destroying the records, but there was a primary school in connection with the academy. Biographies state that she "became an educated and accomplished young woman."[33]

In 1859 the Brazos reservation closed, and Captain Shapley assisted in transferring the Indians—some Comanche, Caddo, Waco, Tawakoni, Tonkawa, Anadarko, splinters of Delaware, Shawnee, Choctaw, and Ioni—to the Indian Territory near present-day Anadarko. He went to San Antonio a while later, but it is not known whether he took his family. He soon returned to Waco.

Some of the Comanches from the Territory continued to raid in Texas. In 1860, Governor Houston commissioned Sul a Ranger captain to "break them" permanently. Captain Sul took forty Rangers, twenty U.S. cavalrymen, and seventy frontiersmen and started after the Indians.[34]

While marching up Peace River, they saw buffalo running toward them. Captain Sul suspected Indians and went to a high hill. About two hundred yards away, Comanches were dismantling a village. Captain Sul signaled his men, who bore down on the campers. During the melee, the Texans killed an old Indian whom they believed to be Chief Peta Nocona, and a fifteen-year-old girl, riding behind him on the horse. They captured thirty-six-year-old Cynthia Ann Parker, the chief's white wife, and her two-year-old daughter Prairie Flower; then Captain Sul picked up a nine-year-old Comanche boy, hiding in the grass crying.[35] A descendant of the chief and other sources say that the man killed was not Nocona, but No-Bah. Nocona was supposedly in the Wichita Mountains with his older son, Quanah.[36]

Furthermore, the descendant says that during her effort to escape, Cynthia Ann had the baby *and* her son, Pecos, on the horse with her. Pecos fell off, and she went on, but was caught.[37] Captain Sul took the boy home with him. One account holds that he took Cynthia Ann and the baby, while another says that he sent her to Camp Cooper, then to her relatives. He could have done both. The baby died soon; Cynthia died "with a broken heart" in 1870.

But who was the Comanche boy Captain Sul picked up? Could he have been Quanah Parker's brother, Pecos? His descendants today do not know what happened to him. Whoever the boy was, he became a foster brother to Lizzie.[38] One can imagine the palaver the two had: the boy discussing the exploits of the Comanches, and Lizzie telling of her new life in the city. They were about the same age.

Captain Sul named the boy "Peace Ross" in reference to the Peace River battle, and allowed him to live on the family plantation. It lay about six miles below Waco on the Brazos River near Flat Creek.[39] Peace was given permission to return to his people, but he chose to remain on the plantation. He married the daughter of a former slave in the Neil McLennan household.[40]

All the while as Rangers, Captains Peter and Sul Ross sought treaties with the Indians. When the Civil War erupted, they felt safe in leaving the Rangers for the Confederacy. By then Captain Sul was married to Miss Tinsley who accompanied him to Mississippi.[41] As most families did during the Civil War, the Rosses in Waco remained static. When Captain Shapley had to be away, Armstead, the dependable slave, and his wife were available. Peter and Sul advanced in the army, with Sul becoming a brigadier general. He fought in 132 battles during which he had six horses shot from under him. Two monuments stand on Vicksburg National Battlefield in his honor. Colonel Peter was wounded twice.

When the two men returned home, General and Mrs. Sul moved to the farm for him to recuperate. Colonel Peter married Laura Harrison, daughter of General James E. Harrison, in 1866.[42] The Waco census for July 5, 1870, listed Charles P. (Shapley) Ross, fifty-nine, a native of Kentucky and a farmer with real estate valued at $15,000 and personal property at $1,000. Katherine Ross, his wife, was fifty-eight and a native of Virginia.

Kate, nineteen, and William, sixteen, were native Texans, while Lizzie, also sixteen, was "Indian" and born in the Indian Territory. This does not coincide with Lizzie's estimated age of "eight" when she was taken from the Comanches. In 1870, she should have been twenty. Someone other than a knowledgeable adult could have reported the census.[43]

Also in the household were Cynthia, twenty-five, a black female and domestic servant, born in Virginia; Louisia, one, and Jane, three and a half, both black females and natives of Texas. They were probably Cynthia's children. In addition, there was Mary J., two, and Charlie (Chaplie) two and a half, Peter's children. His wife, Laura, had died that year. Robert S. and Annie were not listed. Robert married Bettie Glenn in 1870. He, too, had been a captain in the Civil War, then became a publisher of the *Waco Advance* with his brother, William H. Annie, who became Mrs. Patrick Fitzwilliams of California, may have been married at that time.

At least part of the family went west in 1870. Captain Shapley went out for his health, but did not remain long. Peter went to farm and trade for four years, then returned to Waco. Some time during that decade, Mrs. Shapley took Lizzie there on a visit. She married a "wealthy merchant near Los Angeles," where she was living in 1884.[44]

Her rescuer, General Sul, became governor of Texas in 1887 and president of Texas A and M College in 1891. He and Mrs. Ross had six children. He died in 1898.[45]

One writer listed Lizzie's death in 1886, another in 1903. Neither could be verified, for just as the fairy tale's prince remained anonymous, so did Lizzie's "wealthy merchant." And paralleling both Cinderellas' mysterious beginning was their silent "happiness ever after."[46] Thus from a historic tragedy for the Indians came a godsend for Lizzie Ross and a story stranger than any fairy tale.

HERTA HUGE BOHM LUCAS
Naturalized Oklahoman Once Caught in European Crossfire

With another war looming at a "line in the desert" (1991), it seems relevant to turn the calendar back half a century and travel with a victim of World War II in Europe. She is Herta Huge Bohm Lucas, a transplanted Sooner, now of Lawton.[47] Married to Albert Lucas, a native of Holdenville, Oklahoma, she came to the United States with him in 1948. To help her live with the horrors of the past, Herta wrote her experiences in a manuscript,

"Courage: Portrait of a Woman's Survival."[48] To read it is to weep.

Herta was born in Konigsberg, East Prussia, between Lithuania and Poland as the daughter of Lieutenant (later Major) Heinrich and Mrs. Amalie Shuetz Huge. Her father, a mixture of Italian and Prussian, was a descendant from a member of the Pope's family who was an officer in the Prussian Army. His hobby was magic. Herta's mother was a designer in an opera house. The family lived in comfort as High Germans.[49]

Herta attended a girls' school and studied to be a Protestant missionary. She helped her father with his magic, serving as the person who disappeared. In 1940 she married Walter Bohm, an officer in the Prussian Army. They had a military ceremony, but got to be together only on two short furloughs. He was killed in 1942 during the Battle of Stalingrad, more than a thousand miles away. The couple's daughter Marianne was born in the home of Herta's parents in Konigsberg. Walter never saw her. All the while, two armies were coming closer to Konigsberg—the Germans and the Russians.[50]

Herta's mother took Marianne to the family's summer cottage at Rantau on the Baltic sea, which saved them from possible death during the bombing of Konigsberg. Herta, her father, and fifty-one others were in the cellar when bombs crumpled the building on top of them. Herta's hair and face were badly burned. For seven hours they dug to free

Below: Herta Huge Bohm Lucas, now a resident of Lawton, was caught in a crossfire between Germans and Russians during World War II. Her escape was harrowing. (From the author's collection)

themselves. When they finally crawled out, an SS guard drew his gun. "Get back in that cellar," he commanded, "and die for Hitler." Herta's "Papa" Heinrich Huge shot the guard.

Leaving the city in flames, they escaped to their summer cottage and the comfort of "Mama and Marianne." Mama did not recognize Herta. Within a few days, allied planes from Sweden attacked Rantau. Homeless and empty handed, the family escaped into the woods. A farmer gave them shelter, but not for long. The Russian Navy struck from the sea, injuring Herta's parents and Marianne.[51] Papa willed that Herta take the baby and flee to the West. He gave her a package of cigarettes, all he had, and said they would come in handy (as barter). He assured her further she could make it.

"As long as you can chew and swallow," he said, "the spit will keep you alive."[52]

Papa had learned that trick during three years as a prisoner of war in Morocco in World War I. He helped the children to the railroad station. Day after day, as the two rode the refugee train across Poland and Czechoslovakia to Dresden, Germany, Herta had Marianne chew the handle of her purse, and she traded the cigarettes for two slices of bread. At Sebnitz, Herta found relatives. A man thought Marianne was dead, and she looked it, but through Herta's efforts, prayers and the goodness of a few people who gave them food, she survived.[53]

Herta and her relatives began working in a factory where they were forced to fill vials with poison. Her grandfather's hands became so cold he could no longer do the work. A guard knocked him down. When Herta and a relative tried to help him, the guard struck them and took the grandfather away. Papa Heinrich escaped from Prussia and appeared at Sebnitz in rags. He pointed to the hilltop, where he wished to be buried "close to God." Soon he was in the hospital. When Herta went to see him, he lay naked on a board in the basement, the object of torture. She pulled the sheet from a body nearby and spread it over him. His lips parted, exposing his bloody mouth.[54]

"They had pulled his gold teeth," Herta said. "I didn't tell Mama about his suffering. I said he died of exhaustion."[55]

Herta and a relative pulled him on a sled to the funeral home. The kind lady director gave Herta his coat (she had none) and shirt and wrapped him in a sheet. Later, she dressed him in a silk shirt to match the lining of the casket and placed a lavender rose

Herta's survival led to marriage with an American Army sergeant, Albert Lucas, of Holdenville. Herta's mother, Mrs. Huge, was a member of the wedding party in Germany. (Courtesy Herta Huge Bohm Lucas)

in his hand. The family had no flowers for his burial, so they sprinkled a little sand on his casket. "Even though the sun came out on the hilltop Papa had chosen," Herta said, "that was the saddest and loneliest day of my young life."

In 1945 the Russians closed in again, and the family had to flee. Traveling nine days on the train, they suffered from hunger, lice, and the humiliation of having only one pot for everybody. Forced to steal for survival, Herta was jailed at least once and had to pick bugs from potato plants another time.

When caught talking to a Jew, her cousin by marriage, she was put in prison. Two dogs, trained to attack if she moved, forced her to stand motionless for twenty-four hours. She shrank to eighty-seven pounds, "skin and bones," she said. In addition to her own suffering, she grieved for relatives and friends. SS troops beat one of her grandfathers to death for not leaving his home in Konigsberg; then her grandmother died with a heart attack. Some of her family members were gassed at Auschwitz; others were bayonetted, hanged, or raped, and one was thrown from a window and taken to a dump.[56]

The Russians were holding and torturing Herta and a relative when the Americans arrived in 1945 to free them. A short time after the Army of Occupation moved in, she and a relative went searching through their garbage. A soldier came out and asked them if they would like to work. They gladly took a job, and life became brighter.[57]

Among the liberators was Sergeant Albert Lucas. Like many of his fellow Americans who were attracted to the lovely European maidens, he fell in love with Herta and she with him. On October 2, 1948, they were married in two ceremonies—one at the local courthouse and one at church in Bad Kissingen. "I didn't understand a word Albert's chaplain said," Herta laughed, "but when he elbowed me in the side, I said, 'Yes.'"

They came to the United States and settled at Lawton-Fort Sill. Master Sergeant Lucas retired in 1962 and entered construction work. The couple's daughter Marianne married David E. Riley of Cashion. They now live in Oklahoma City and have a son, Carey.

Despite the atrocities Herta suffered during the war, she is a happy, delightful person who can laugh at the cultural and language blunders she made while becoming an American. And she is forever thankful for life, for Albert, her family and freedom. She hopes there will never be another war.[58]

****

Paradoxically, a scattering of women captives through the ages became leaders of their people—authorities. Esther of Bible fame became the wife of King Xerxes and the liberator of her people. Then there were free women who became rulers: Catherine the Great of Russia and Queen Victoria of England. The latter's position included Empress of India. There has never been a woman chief executive of the United States or of Oklahoma, but Native American women have been rulers of their tribes for centuries. They still are with much success.

43

Chapter 5
AUTHORITIES

MILDRED IMACHE CLEGHORN
(1910-   )
Born a Prisoner of War

Whether in her tribal headquarters near Apache, Oklahoma, appearing on television for the Smithsonian Institution in Washington, D.C., or administering to women in the Fiji Islands, Mildred I. Cleghorn conducts her "royal" duties with dedication but with a common touch. She is chairperson (chief) of the once-feared Fort Sill Apache Indian tribe.[1] The first woman of her tribe to hold that position, Mildred was the choice of her people in 1977 and has continued to be so ever since, as confirmed by the latest vote in 1991. Prior to being chosen for her present position, she served in numerous auxiliary offices.[2]

Tall and with long, straight hair wound into a silver bun on top of her head, she rises to greet the public with the grace and strength of an eagle. Her brown eyes twinkle, as a submerged smile plays across her bronzed face. She extends a hand.[3] One feels a genuine welcome and is cognizant of the lady's stately posture and tasteful dress. A cascade of coral-colored beads over her bodice matches the print in her long gray blouse and befitting skirt. Her poise and friendliness denote leadership and a readiness to communicate.[4] So, what is the story of this Indian woman of note? How was she able to get this far and stay so long?

Born a POW (prisoner of war) at Fort Sill, Oklahoma, Mildred's parents, Amy and Richard Imache, also, were POWs. Her father was seven years old when he and his family were taken in 1886. That was during the United States Army's pursuit of Geronimo (Goyathe or "One-Who-Yawns").[5] He and his band of Chiricahua Apaches surrendered in Mexico and were sent to prison in Florida. Two years later, they were transferred to Alabama where Mildred's mother was born.

In 1894, the United States government returned them to Fort Sill. Part of the Apaches elected to go to the Mescalero Reservation in New Mexico, while the Imaches chose to stay in Geronimo's circle at Fort Sill. Both groups remained prisoners until 1913.[6]

Those last years as prisoners, Geronimo and his group lived under guard in small houses on Fort Sill's East Range, farmed small patches, and raised stock.[7] That was the tribe's situation when Mildred Imache Cleghorn was born, three years before the Apaches were freed. As soon as she reached school age, she started her education.[8] Mildred, with the encouragement of her parents, graduated from Apache, Oklahoma, High School, then entered Haskell Institute at Lawrence, Kansas. From there she went to Cameron Junior College (now Cameron University) in Lawton, Oklahoma, after which she earned a bachelor's degree at Oklahoma State University, working for part of her support. She did graduate study there and at the University of Oklahoma in Norman.[9] The young woman married Bill

Below: This stately, white-haired lady, Mildred Imache Cleghorn, was born a prisoner of war at Fort Sill, Oklahoma, and remained so three years. She grew up to win many honors, including becoming chief of her tribe. (Courtesy Mildred Imache Cleghorn)

Mildred Imache Cleghorn visits with another indomitable Oklahoma woman, Lucille Taylor Pintz. The two worked with Indian youths in the West during the same years. (Taken by the author)

Cleghorn, a coach at Anadarko, Oklahoma. He died in 1970.[10]

Broadening her education, Mildred went on several tours: to England and Europe, to Oaxaca, Mexico, to Alaska and Berlin. Her most extensive tour was worldwide, including the Fiji Islands, Australia, and New Zealand. The latter was sponsored by Church Women United of the United States. It was in behalf of women's circumstance everywhere.[11] Mildred's early professional work was that of clerk-typist. She later became a home economist, teacher, and counselor. She worked with kindergarten-age children, adolescents, and adults in Oklahoma, Wisconsin, Nevada, Kansas, and New Mexico and administered to women around the world.[12]

Mildred has served on numerous boards, agencies, and corporations locally, statewide, and nationally. To mention a few, they include: the Association of South Central Oklahoma Government; the Consistory of the Apache Reformed Church ("the first woman of our church"); advisor for Caddo-Kiowa Area Vo-Tech programs; and Science and Education workshop conductor, Mobile, Alabama.[13] Also, General Program Council of Reformed Church of America; National Association of University Women of Oklahoma; Salvation Army Committee; Indian Health Advisory Board; National Congress of American Indians; Campfire Counselor; and Morning Star Foundation of Washington D.C.[14]

The lady takes time to follow her hobby, which has brought her national acclaim. She creates au-

thentically dressed Indian dolls. They have been on exhibit at the First and Tenth Annual Folklore Festival, Smithsonian Institution, Washington, D.C.; at the Turtle Museum, Niagara Falls, New York; and the Indian Summer Festival in Milwaukee, Wisconsin. The dolls have been on traveling exhibits in Oklahoma and other places.[15] They were the subject of a cover story in *Future Homemakers of Oklahoma* magazine and were the subject of discussion during Mildred's appearance on the telecast for the Smithsonian Institution, which was aired on OETA, Channel 13, Oklahoma City, during the summer of 1991.[16]

Mildred's honors and awards are multiple. Her four fellowships came from Fisk University, Nashville, Tennessee; the University of Texas, Austin; a nutrition seminar, Bangalore, India; a World Tour; and a White House conference. She was "Outstanding Elementary Teacher," "Outstanding Indian" at the American Indian Exposition, Anadarko, Oklahoma, and recipient of the Diamond 4-H pin for twenty years leadership in that organization. She received the Ellis Island "Medal of Honor," was "Honored Guest" at the Centennial of the Cessation of Hostilities between the Chiricahua Apaches and the United States at Bowie, Arizona, and at the site of Geronimo's surrender in Cañon de los Embudos, Mexico.[17] A completely different honor was her appearance in the Rose Bowl parade as one of eight Apache Chieftain Equestrian group. They were in full ceremonial regalia. That was in 1989. A further honor: she was featured in *National Geographic* magazine in 1992.[18]

When Mildred Imache Cleghorn was in school, did she encounter any prejudices? "Not as much as today," she said. "Many speak of my people as 'them old drunk Indians, too lazy to work.' We do have some problems, but we are trying to do something about them."[19]

What has been the highlight of Mildred's career? "My work on the reservation (in New Mexico)," she said. Why was that? "Because I saw the great need," she answered, "not only for the children, but for adults as well."

What does she consider her greatest contribution to her tribe? "Acquiring this two-and-a-half-acre plot," she said, "and this tribal complex. There are four buildings for service to my people."[20] They include the headquarters, decorated with Indian art and sculpture; an activity building; a shelter; and a dining room.

What are her plans for the future? "To maintain what we have," she said, "to promote economic development, and keep our identity as a tribe. We're starting a new language class to perpetuate tribal traditions. Our people are scattered from New York to Washington state, Mississippi, and even Australia. We get many queries about ancestors, and we want to be able to answer them. We want to keep our identity, also."[21]

Mildred lives near Apache, Oklahoma, with her adopted daughter Penny, recently returned from a job in Germany.

ALICE BROWN DAVIS
(1852-1935)
Chief of the Seminoles

Alice Brown Davis did it all. She bore eleven children, supervised the family ranch after her husband's death, cooked for twenty cowboys, operated a trading post and post office at Arbeka, Indian Territory, and taught and superintended schools. She served as interpreter, disbursed payments to Seminole soldiers after the Civil War, served as chief and counselor to her tribesmen, and read the Bible every day.[22]

Chief Davis had somewhat of a "royal" heritage. Her father, Dr. John F. Brown, was a Scotsman born in South Carolina but educated at the University of Edinburgh in Scotland. The United States government appointed him to accompany the Seminoles from the Florida Everglades to Indian Territory in the late 1830s.[23] On that long trek, which meant death for many and suffering for most, Dr. Brown had the good fortune to meet Lucy Redbird of the noted Tiger clan of the Seminoles. The couple fell in love. Disregarding tribal opposition to mixing their race, the doctor and Lucy were married.[24] Their first home was at Tahlequah, where some contingents of the tribe landed. One of their eight children was Alice. She had a private Cherokee tutor and learned very fast.[25]

By 1856 the Seminoles had been assigned a section of land west of the Creeks. It reached to the 100th meridian, now the western border of Oklahoma. A few years later, they established a council house on Greenhead prairie about six miles northeast of present-day Wanette, in Pottawatomie County. The tribe had a commissary, blacksmith shop, and later a school.[26] The Civil War (1861-1865) scattered the tribe. Some of the young men

entered the army. Others went to Kansas, to Ft. Gibson, or into the Chickasaw nation as refugees.

After the war, Dr. Brown moved his family from Tahlequah to the Seminole Capitol-Council House and continued practicing medicine. His oldest son, John, Jr., opened a store.[27]

The Seminoles were hardly over the war when a cholera epidemic struck. This, with all the other diseases, placed a great burden on Dr. Brown. Alice became his helper, but even that was not enough relief. Dr. Brown died of exhaustion, and soon thereafter his widow Lucy died.[28]

Because all Five Civilized Tribes entered the Civil War on the Confederate side and lost, part of their penalty was loss of land—the entire western section. The United States government took it for reservations and placed the Wild Tribes there. That meant that the Seminoles had to move their border nearer the Creeks.[29] It meant also that they had to

Below: This bust of Seminole Chief Alice Brown Davis, whose deeds were countless, is in the Indian Hall of Fame at Anadarko. (Taken by the author)

fraud. In addition, they were granted monetary awards. Bentley and the Wolves reaped at least a portion of that which they had sown.[55]

Overshadowed by the prolonged conspiracy against them, the two Kickapoo chiefs faded from accounts of the turmoils several years. Then Wah-Pah-Ho-Ko's group showed up in Sonora, Mexico, near Douglas, Arizona. Impoverished and hopeless, they appealed to the government, received help, and returned to Oklahoma in the 1920s.[56] By that time, all the tribes in Oklahoma had been integrated into the state and national societies.

Records relative to Wah-Pah-Ho-Ko's life and family are practically nil. One man in Muzquiz, Mexico, claimed to be her grandson.

At least one other Indian woman became a chief in Indian Territory. She was Rosana Chouteau, an Osage, in 1875. She is featured in Carolyn Foreman's book, *Indian Women Chiefs*, published by Star Printery, Inc., Muskogee, 1953.[57] (Sources of information on all subjects in this book may be found in the appendix.)

WILMA MANKILLER SOAP
(1945-   )
First Woman Chief of the Cherokees

Wilma Mankiller is a fighter. She has lived in a battle zone practically all of her life and, at age 46 (1991), is still conquering territory.[58] Mankiller wears the armor of serenity, idealism, determination...for which she paid a high price. She dashes from one problem, program, or project to another. They are centered in her nation—that of the Cherokees—but are not confined to its boundaries.[59]

As chief of her tribe for the third time, and the first woman to hold that office, she arises early at her ancestral home on Mankiller Flats, Rocky Mountain community, near Stilwell, Oklahoma, and drives to her office in the Cherokee Headquarters at Tahlequah.[60] Often she goes on to the local airport to take the tribal plane to Oklahoma City, Washington, D.C., or elsewhere.[61]

Her duties at home include supervision of a $50 million budget, a thousand workers, medical and literacy services, the Cherokee Heritage Center including the theater for Tsa-La-Gi, and the Cherokee museum and ancient village. She also oversees businesses and industries, such as apartment complexes, motels, restaurants, a hydroelectric plant, and gift shops along with encouraging her people to become more self-sufficient.[62] Away from the nation, Mankiller presents programs, seeks grants, intercedes for her tribesmen—the list is endless. There are constant demands on her time and expertise. Then it is back home to be wife, mother of five children, and grandmother to several others.

Wilma's battles began, one might say, at her birth, but she was unaware of them for a few years. One of eleven children, she is the offspring of a Dutch-Irish mother and a full-blood Cherokee father, Irene and Charlie Mankiller. She was born November 16, 1945, in the Indian hospital at Tahlequah, Oklahoma.[63] World War II was just over, but whatever prosperity peace generated in the country did not filter into the Cherokee Nation. Although stream-slashed and humped with timbered hills, the rocky country suffered drought. The usual strawberries, beans, and peanuts failed to produce. Jobs elsewhere became unavailable. Farm families suffered.[64]

The BIA (Bureau of Indian Affairs) decided to scatter the drought-stricken families into metropolitan areas. The Mankillers settled in a ghetto-type neighborhood of San Francisco, California. Mankiller's father became a longshoreman and organizer, but one salary was inadequate, and living with strangers was no comfort. There was only one other Cherokee family in the area.[65] Wilma found the change both shocking and educational. The family had indoor plumbing, electricity, and sirens of emergency vehicles. The neighborhood was tough and poverty-ridden. The future chief, however, managed to graduate from San Francisco State University. She married a wealthy Ecuadorian businessman and had two daughters, Gina Olaya and Felicia Swake. The marriage did not last.[66]

In 1969, a group of Indian activists occupied the abandoned Federal prison on Alcatraz Island to publicize their poverty and seek better treatment. Wilma joined the group. The island of solid rock was a mile from the mainland and had a notorious history.[67] In 1868, it had become a military institution for prisoners serving long sentences. They included Indian chiefs, often imprisoned for defending their territory. After it became a Federal prison in 1934, only the most dangerous criminals were placed there. By 1963 it had become too expensive to maintain, so the government abandoned it.

The experience as an activist at Alcatraz awakened Wilma to the power of politics and its far-

Wilma Mankiller Soap, chief of the Cherokees, lived in a battle zone practically all her life—and is still conquering territory. (Courtesy Cherokee Nation)

reaching ramifications.[68] The Indians made their point and moved out in 1971. That same year, Wilma's father died. In time she felt the need to change her own lifestyle and came to the conclusion that the best way to do that was to change locations. She brought her daughters back to the ancestral home near Stilwell, Oklahoma.[69]

She volunteered to work for her tribe. This led to a job as economic stimulus coordinator. Wilma concentrated on improving conditions in the rural areas. From Bunch to Bushyhead and throughout the fourteen counties of the Cherokee lands, towns were becoming ghost-ridden. Homes were falling into disrepair. People were trapped in doubt and inertia.[70] The future chief succeeded in getting grants for training programs and establishing businesses. There were woodcutting and burning projects, garden raisings, and training in carpentry, plumbing, electricity, and home improvement.[71]

With a desire to improve her own abilities while working with others, Wilma enrolled in the University of Arkansas at Fayetteville to study community

planning. She became a graduate assistant.[72] In 1979, black days fell upon her. While returning from the University, she was almost fatally injured in a car wreck, suffering broken legs and ribs and a badly crushed face. The doctors doubted that she would ever walk again.[73]

The battle to recover included repair to chest and legs and facial plastic surgery. Months later, when she was about to recover, myasthenia gravis, more commonly known as "creeping paralysis," struck her. The medicine she took did not heal her. She became depressed and consulted tribal medicine men.[74] Considered "healers and spiritual counselors," they advocated restoration of harmony from inside out. They displayed the "sacred wampum belts, that teach truth about Cherokee life."[75]

Wilma was on a life-support system when she became angry. She demanded release, took control of her own body, and began to heal. She said that she "became calmer and tougher," then went back to work.[76] Although her physical problems lingered, Wilma was elected deputy chief in 1983. Her people's confidence and admiration and those of others, no doubt, helped her to recover completely.

Honors and awards showered upon her. They included:[77] a citation for Outstanding Contributions to American Leadership and Native American Culture from Harvard University, a doctor's degree in Humane Letters from the University of New England, election as American Indian Woman of the Year by the Oklahoma Federation of Indian Women, nomination to the Oklahoma Women's Hall of Fame by the Governor's Advisory Committee, and the granting of an Honorary Doctorate of Public Service by Rhode Island College.[78] In addition, Wilma was appointed to the Advisory Board for Cornell University, presented the ByLiner's Award by WICI (Women in Communications International) of Oklahoma City, named San Francisco State Alumna of the Year and Woman of the Year by *Ms* magazine, plus several other honors.

In 1983, Wilma was elected deputy chief of her tribe. Ross Swimmer was chief. Two years later the United States government chose him to be deputy Secretary of the Interior in charge of the BIA. That appointment automatically put Wilma at the top of the Cherokees.[79] There were doubts in some circles that a woman could handle that prestigious job, but Wilma knew the tribal history. When they lived beyond the Mississippi River, the Cherokees were a matrilineal society. There were "clan mothers" who shared political power with men. The practice was sometimes referred to as "petticoat government." Women trained the men and even went to war with them.[80] After the tribe came west, it patterned its government after that of the United States. There was no place at the time for women.

More determined to prove herself and help her people, Wilma dug deeper into the duties of her office. In 1987, she was elected chief of the Cherokee Nation. More duties were added to her work load. Then black days fell upon her again.[81] Wilma suffered with a kidney problem and had to have a transplant. That was in 1990. Again she overcame the illness and was reelected chief of the Cherokees in 1991.[82]

Wilma has appeared on numerous TV and radio programs, including "Good Morning America," and has been featured in nationwide publications such as *Southern Living*, *Southern Style*, *Newsweek*, *Ms*, *The American Way*, *Update* (Southern Bell Corporation publication), *Cherokee Nation Communications*, and *Rural News*. With such recognition, she is sure to be outstanding in Cherokee history.[83]

What does she dislike most about being chief?

According to *Southern Living*, Mankiller finds "playing politics in Washington, D.C., most unappealing." She prefers staying home and "tackling situations with a straightforward approach." The chief wants her people to improve their own economy, health, and lifestyle while maintaining their heritage, and she wants them to teach their own history.[84]

Wilma and her husband, Charlie Soap, continue to live in her modest ancestral home. He also works for the Cherokee people.

****

Since the beginning of history, most women have been religious and generous. Hannah of the Old Testament worked and prayed for a son, vowing to consecrate him to Yahweh. She got the son, named him Samuel and gave him to the Lord. In the New Testament Luke told about Lydia, a woman of God, as were Lois and Eunice who were mentioned by Paul. In America, numerous women from the North and East came to Indian Territory as missionaries. The adventures of four such caring women follow. One is a philanthropist.

Chapter 6
MISSIONARIES AND A PHILANTHROPIST

ISABEL CRAWFORD
(1865-1942+)
Canadian Missionary in Kiowa Country

Isabel Crawford, a beautiful and cultured young woman of twenty-eight, ventured into Oklahoma Territory about 1892 and introduced herself to the untamed, nomadic Kiowas, recently transplanted to a reservation. She slept in tepees with the women and dogs and ate what the Indians ate: "sorry pork, beans, applesauce and occasionally beef."[1] Sometimes she had "only bread and syrup" and on one occasion "roast puppy."

The reason for this latter incident was that her host, Lucius Aitsan, was called away and took the wagon, leaving her hostess, Mable Saunt Aitsan, and her without transportation. The trading post was twenty-five miles away.[2] Aitsan, a former student at the famous Indian School in Carlisle, Pennsylvania, had been a soldier in the U.S. Army and was a Christian. He held the job of farmer for the Indian agent and had to be gone on business. When Mable began preparing the puppy, Isabel's stomach revolted, but she grew so hungry she said to her hostess, "If you will scrape off all the hair, I will try the back legs."[3]

The saddest thing Isabel said she experienced, was burials according to ancient rites. Men and women cut off their hair and fingers and gashed their limbs and bodies. They buried the deceaseds' personal belongings with them, drove their animals to the grave sites, and shot them.[4] Some placed their dead upon scaffolds and left them until the fowls picked them to skeletons. (These same customs are mentioned in the Bible and are still practiced by the Parsis in India. This religious group in Bombay uses Towers of Silence for such disposal of the dead.)[5] Isabel made coffins and often helped dig graves. That was for Christian Indians, whose burial customs were the same as those of the whites.[6]

About 1900 the Kiowa women organized a missionary society, and to Isabel's surprise the men wanted to attend. She wrote the Baptist Home Mission Board in Chicago and received permission for them to do so. The men's interest in such activities as quilting surprised her even more.[7]

When allotments were forced upon the Indians at the turn of the 20th century, the Kiowas around Saddle Mountain were granted eighty acres for a church building. This was in addition to their individual allotments. The "surplus" land was divided into 160-acre plots, and white people drew for them in 1901. Isabel ministered to those white settlers, also. At Christmas, 1902, she received eighteen wagonloads of material for distribution at the mission.

A year later on Easter Sunday, the church at Saddle Mountain was finished, and she conducted the first service there. This inspired her to write,[8]

Below: Isabel Crawford, a young Canadian, came to Kiowa country as a missionary at the turn of the century and won their love and protection. (Courtesy Hugh Corwin)

At right, Isabel Crawford conversing with her interpreter Lucius Aitsan, left. Isabel organized and served a church for Kiowas at Saddle Mountain, near Mountain View at the turn of the century. (Courtesy Hugh Corwin)

"Never in my life in civilized America have I seen and felt the power of the Gospel of Jesus Christ, as I have among the blanket Indians of Oklahoma Territory."

Although Isabel was a bona fide missionary, she could not administer such sacraments as the "Jesus eat" (the Lord's supper). Only an ordained minister could do that. She encouraged the church members to call a pastor. They did not want to lose her, but mission authorities sent a man, Harry Treat.[9] In 1906 Isabel retired and returned to Canada to lecture and write about Indians, whom she considered as being "among the noblest and most successful" of all people. One of her greatest joys was when Lucius Aitsan became an ordained minister.[10]

The daughter of a professor, Isabel was educated in a Baptist training school in Chicago. She was still living in 1942. The Saddle Mountain church building is now in Eagle Park, a museum of historic buildings, at Cache, Oklahoma.[11]

ANNA HIEBERT GOMEZ
(1883- ?)
Russian Refugee—Missionary to the Indians

A native of Russia, Anna Hiebert joined the Beckers, also from Russia, at the Mennonite Brethren's Post Oak Mission near Indiahoma in the early 1900s. At that time, Anna was an assistant in the home and in the church.[12]

Most Indians still lived in tents or tepees and cooked much of their scanty food in the open. They dressed in primitive clothing, characteristic to their individual tribe. Many of the men wore long braids, entwined with colored yarn or fur.[13] Polygamy was common and polyandry occurred once in a while. Quanah Parker had seven or eight wives, whereas the norm was two or three. During an interview in 1950, Anna told of a woman who had three husbands. They all lived in the same camp and "got along well." The woman was one of a few who had a house. If one of the husbands arrived while another was there, he waited on the porch until the predecessor left.

The usual marriage custom was to take and keep. Anna said she never knew of an Indian deserting a wife he had taken to his home. One old warrior told Anna that Indians learned desertion, along with drunkenness, from white men. After the arrival of missionaries, the Indians began accepting monogamy—one wife, one husband.

When Anna first came to Post Oak, "responses to church services were discouraging. Often distressing. Only a few Indians attended," she said, "and most of them were sadly lacking in reverence. One old fellow almost invariably started a loud conversation, while the preacher was delivering his sermon. Others stretched out on the benches," she continued, "and went to sleep. They snored every breath. Children and dogs ran in and out, yelling and yelping. In time, services grew in attendance and with considerably more reverence."[14]

Anna said Indians spoke of the church building as the "Jesus House," the preacher as the "Jesus man" and the communion as the "Jesus eat."[15] She remembered, "In the early days, most Indian women refused to go to the hospital, either during illness or childbirth. They had their babies freely and naturally, sometimes alone. All the pomp and precautions about sanitation were just so much nonsense to them. One woman, for instance," she said, "attended a camp meeting one night until about eleven o'clock, had her baby, then got up next morning and cooked breakfast.[16] The younger women," Anna chuckled, "welcome the hospital. They like its cleanliness, its antiseptic odor and good food. Some want to stay indefinitely.

"Another change," Anna noted, "was in the Indians' relation to their dead. In the early days, they harbored primitive superstitions about spirits returning, so they destroyed everything belonging to the deceased.[17] They rushed to the mission with the bodies, sometimes before the persons had drawn their last breath, and placed them in a small house used as a type of funeral home. All night they sat around a campfire, beating tom-toms in a low weird rhythm and chanted in muffled tones."

Instead of offering flowers, they showered the open grave with their shawls and hats. Sometimes there were twelve to fifteen beautifully embroidered shawls and as many hats in a grave. Also buried with the dead were jewelry, pottery, clothing, money and personal effects. Larger items, such as bed covers used by the deceased, were burned and their horses shot.[18]

Below: Anna Hiebert Gomez, born in Russia, came to Post Oak Mission near Indiahoma as a missionary to the Comanches early this century. She is shown here with her husband, Joe Gomez, another missionary, who came from Mexico. (Courtesy the Gomez family)

The belief that a large sum of money was buried with Chief Quanah Parker led to the robbery of his grave at Post Oak Cemetery. Anna recalled the incident, "For two nights before the robbery's discovery," she said "I saw a lantern in the cemetery. I mentioned it the following mornings to other missionaries. They laughed and teased me about seeing ghosts. I realized later I should have pressed for an investigation. The robbers got nothing," she said, "except two silver dollars. They had been placed on the old chief's eyes. His diamond stickpin was left. He got a second burial."[19] He is now resting on Chief's Knoll in Fort Sill's cemetery.

Anna was the daughter of German (Dutch) parents, Mr. and Mrs. Hiebert. Her birthplace was Kime near Odessa and the Black Sea. She attended schools there four years before leaving at age ten. She remembered Russia and the stories her family told of their flights from place to place.[20] Because of oppression, her ancestors and many other Anabaptists fled the Spanish Netherlands to Prussia. There they reclaimed swampland and made great progress as "quiet, industrious people." Oppression plus exorbitant taxes compelled them to seek another homeland.[21] Empress Catherine II of Russia offered the zealots land, religious freedom and exemption from military duty in her country. They took it and worked hard to earn the privileges.

Eventually, political change eclipsed those privileges. By then, the Hieberts were wealthy mill operators in Russia. A break in a dam washed away their property. The country's officials launched an investigation. They discovered a large sum of water-soaked money in the bricks of the Hiebert home and confiscated it. The family was left destitute.[22] The Hieberts began teaching and preaching. The Russians launched persecutions against them and others of the same faith. This drove many of them back to Germany and finally to America. Some of the Hieberts' friends went to India.[23]

In America Anna studied for mission work in Chicago and in Gotebo, Oklahoma, then joined the Beckers at Post Oak. She married Joe Gomez, a missionary from Mexico. They had five children, all raised at the mission.[24]

At age sixty-seven, Anna was going strong. She did her own housework and laundry, drove the car full of Indians on missions of mercy and business, made public appearances at church and social gatherings, and hosted large numbers of Indians and missionaries. During one holiday season, she helped cook for thirty-six people. And yet, she declared she had done nothing to write about. "It's all in a day's work," she declared.[25]

Even though she suffered hardships as a child, Anna thought these might have better prepared her for a missionary career. The plain little woman, short and stocky in stature, was as natural as the prairie where she dwelt. She was free from sham and pretense and taught her children to be likewise. They became missionaries or devout workers in the church.[26]

ANNA KLYDE BENNETT DAVIS
(1897-1982)
Gave Her Own Eulogy

Imagine going half a world away from the United States to shoot your first Roman candle on the Fourth of July. Imagine at the same time being a so-called "senior citizen" with angina pectoris while far from family, friends, and familiarity.[27] That was the lot of Anna Klyde Bennett Davis in 1966. She was on the Island of Penang, Malaysia, in the Strait of Malacca. She did not go there to shoot fireworks. She went as a missionary for the Church of Christ, and the celebration was for all Americans living there at the time.[28]

Held at the home of the USIS Director, with whom the missionaries had to register, the festivities included a covered dish dinner on the lawn—1914 style. The burst of fireworks and patriotism in that faraway land was an annual affair, where strangers were not strangers any more. Klyde went there after she lost her beloved husband, Dr. E.O. Davis. For some time, she thought *her* life was over. At an age and in a state of health when most people take to rockers and reminiscing, what else could she do but follow suit? But she did not want that.[29]

Born in Texas, Klyde came to Asher, Oklahoma, with her family when she was a child. She attended local schools and married young. The couple had four children: A.E., Carleta, Max and Peggy. Klyde's only interest outside of home, family, and helping the doctor was church work. An excellent Bible student, she had been teaching and lecturing since she became a Christian at age seventeen. Her children grew up in Asher, married, and scattered into four different states.[30]

The couple moved to Lawton where the doctor practiced and she assisted until his retirement, then they went to Madill. Both threw themselves whole-

heartedly into church and humanitarian work. Like Lydia in the book of Acts, Klyde's devotion and ability became known far and wide. Then it happened. She became a widow. Her loss brought her low. She groped in loneliness and indecision, trying to find new directions.[31]

In 1965 a minister friend, Lloyd Smith of Dallas, contacted Klyde to go to Asia as a missionary. She would grade correspondence papers and teach Bible to the youth of Malaysia. The challenge quickened her. What an opportunity! Her will said "Go!" Circumstances said "No!"[32] Klyde had never been out of the United States. She had never flown in a plane. She would be among complete strangers whose native language and culture she did not know. Her children would never agree to her going, and most everybody else would brand her "Crazy!" She wrestled with the desire, finally deciding, "I'll go!"[33]

In January 1966 she boarded a plane in Dallas for San Francisco where she met a missionary family, the Greens. They were going to the Far East. Together they spent two days in Tokyo, Japan, two in Saigon, Vietnam, within hearing distance of war, and two in Bangkok, Thailand, before going on to Malaysia. Some other American missionaries met them in Kuala Lumpur, the capital, and took them to Sereman. Klyde worked there and in Ipoh before settling down on Penang. There she had an apartment and office in the same building which housed the church. She shared work with another American couple, Mr. and Mrs. H.O. Jenks, and a Chinese

Below: Anna Klyde Bennett Davis stands before a Bible class of young listeners on Penang, an island off the coast of Malaysia in the 1960s. (Courtesy Klyde Davis)

minister, Ming Paul Lee, who lived upstairs with his mother.[34]

Happily, Klyde found many people spoke English. That was a carry-over from the days when the Malay Peninsula was part of the British Empire. She began learning conversational Chinese from her new friends and taking instructions in Malay.[35] Day by day she came in close contact with the many ethnic groups whose customs were not only strange but often perturbing: Hindus, Buddhists, Mohammedans, Confucianists, Sikhs, and animists (those who believe that inanimate objects and material phenomena possess a soul; another name is "nature worshippers"). And there also were Christians of various denominations. She learned to respect and cope with all of them.[36]

"They were great on meditation," Klyde said.

Her job of teaching and grading Bible lessons kept her busy many hours a day—sometimes far into the night. Up to 6,000 people were enrolled in five different courses at a time. Added to that, a constant stream of people came to the mission for consultation and material help. She found time, however, to see some of the island and mainland and to learn as well as teach. In the vicinity were churches, mosques, temples of various kinds. And most every family had a shrine in the house or yard. At an Indian temple on special days, penitent celebrants inserted wire cages into their flesh and marched in parades. They shed no blood. Another startling feat, they walked on beds of live coals seemingly without being burned.[37]

At another temple, worshippers burned paper images of houses, automobiles, and money for their deceased ancestors' spiritual use. In another, the zealots worshipped snakes, of which many occupied the temple. Klyde recoiled when a little girl told her,[38] "I came with Father today, when he brought an offering to the snakes."

Klyde watched funeral rites. Long processions wound through the streets. Paid participants mourned, beat percussion instruments, and performed acrobatics. She attended weddings. One depressing ceremony united an aged man, crippled and with only one eye, to a girl of nineteen. He paid a thousand dollars for her.

After spending two and a half years on Penang, Klyde returned home for ten months. Her Asian friends begged her to return. She was ready. The second time, she stayed twenty months.[39] Life was not always exciting or successful. The government

On the back row, second from right, Anna Klyde Bennett Davis poses with members of the church she was serving on Penang, an island in the Bay of Bengal, Indian Ocean. (Courtesy Klyde Davis)

allowed the teaching of Western religion only to nationalities other than Malays. Some took the correspondence courses anyway. When one young man became a Christian, he had to leave the country. He went to Singapore, an island-nation off the southern tip of Malaysia.

The role of women distressed Klyde. Not only were they sold like buffalo and chickens, but the Mohammedan women were not allowed in the mosques. They were said to "defile" holy places.[40] When this writer went to Malaysia, the guide took both men and women into the mosque. "You women," he said, "have a privilege our women do not have. They have to pray at home."

One of Klyde's biggest battles was with herself. She had to rest when she wanted to be working. Furthermore she contacted dengue fever, known as "bone-break fever." Caused by a mosquito bite, it is said to affect the victim as though his bones were literally breaking. For two months Klyde was an outpatient at a hospital.[41] During that time, a Chinese Christian girl, Lim Ming Ai, from Singapore came to help her grade papers. Mrs. Lee prepared her meals. People came from as far away as Kuala Lumpur, to see Klyde and receive instructions.[42] "I couldn't go to them," she said, "so they came to me. Some of my best friends I have in this world are Asians."

After almost six years in that exotic world, Klyde returned to live in Shawnee. She was planning another missionary journey, this time a short one to South Africa, when she learned she had cancer. Refusing to take chemotherapy, she accepted fate as it came. Klyde's attitude was so remarkable, a program director from a TV station asked to interview her on tape. She agreed.[43]

Daughters Carleta from Colorado and Peggy from Pennsylvania prepared their mother for the interview. Propped up in bed and smiling, she answered questions about her life and what it was like to face death.[44] Throughout the interview, she was cheerful and expressed her readiness to go. Like the Apostle Paul, Klyde had "fought a good fight...a crown was laid up" for her.

Death was not immediate, so the daughters, both telephone operators and mothers, had to return home. When the "curtain" dropped, sons A.E. from Houston, Texas, and Dr. Max from Edmond came to her side. Both were educators. Included in Klyde's memorial services was the tape of her TV interview.[45] Paraphrasing the scriptures, Hebrews 11:4, one might say that Anna Klyde Bennett Davis, "being dead, yet spoke."

LOUISE DAVIS McMAHAN
(1874-1966)
Philanthropist and Promoter of Culture

"Those who joy would win must share it; happiness was born a twin."[46] Louise Davis McMahan quoted that statement from Lord Byron in her memoirs, *Reminiscences and Scrapbook*. She proved she believed it in her deeds, kindness and generosity, but most of all in the promotion and aggrandizement of her son's memorial—the McMahan Foundation of Lawton, Oklahoma.[47]

The two set it up in 1940 in honor of their husband and father, E.P. McMahan, who died in 1936. The initial sum of the Foundation was $50,000, but Louise and son Eugene added to it regularly.[48] An early Board of Trustees included Lawrence Keegan, W.F. Barber, Ned Shepler, John Shoemaker, and the McMahans. At first, gifts from the interest were small. They went to such places as City Mission, the fire department for a resuscitator, and the Negro Mission. As funds increased, scholarships went to journalism students, to destitute and sick individuals, churches, schools, museums, and numerous other public institutions.[49]

In 1945, Eugene died, leaving the bulk of his fortune to the Foundation. Living in San Antonio since 1926, but keeping Lawton connections, Louise took her son there to bury him beside his father.[50] She decided then that it was time for her to move back and finance a building for the Foundation. The site was 714-716 C Avenue, where the family home had stood since 1901.[51]

Jennie McCutcheon became her secretary and prepared Louise's memoirs for publication. She wrote of her employer's humanitarian deeds and disposition, and also of her philanthropies.

Louise's background was one of note. Born in St. Joseph, Missouri, she was the daughter of John and Martha Reynolds Davis. When she was "an infant in arms," the Davises moved to Clyde, Kansas. That was in 1874.[52] Some people still lived in dugouts, but Mr. Davis managed to get a four-room plank house. He bought hides and sold them to Leavenworth Prison for inmates to make into shoes and boots. He prospered, built a two-story brick house and used the first floor for a store.

The couple had two boys—Jim and Chad. When they grew large enough to do the milking, they quarreled over whose turn it was to perform this chore. Mr. Davis bought another cow so each boy would have a cow to milk every day.[53]

On a visit to St. Joseph in 1882, the Davises noticed that the townspeople were in shock. They had just learned that their neighbor, who had been shot in the back by a house guest, was not Thomas Howard, as they had known him. He was Jesse James. Louise remembered the house on the hill where the murder occurred.[54] Many people there, she said, sympathized with the James brothers. They talked about the savage treatment Union troops had heaped upon the James brothers' mother, who had lost an arm.

Mr. Davis became a shoe salesman. The children finished the Clyde school, which ended at grade ten, and Louise entered Camden Point Christian College in Missouri. She studied music, art, and a few other subjects. She finished in two years and went home. There she found that things were different.[55] E.P. McMahan, a handsome, twenty-four-year-old man from Wisconsin, was superintendent of schools. He had added two more years to the high school program, bringing it up to twelve. Louise wanted to attend a year, take the teachers' examination and teach in the country.

She took her records from Camden Point and asked Superintendent McMahan to enroll her in subjects to qualify her for the teachers' examination. Being a lawyer as well as an educator, perhaps, prompted him to question her in detail about Camden Point.[56] A bit testy, Louise recited the school's history in detail. She waited. Instead of a compliment on her knowledge, McMahan said that she would have to take an examination before he could place her. She walked out.

That evening Superintendent McMahan went to the Davis home to consult with and advise the girl's parents. The three of them changed her plan of action. She enrolled in eleventh-grade subjects. But she and the superintendent had another clash.[57]

He asked her to describe a Leyden jar (a device for accumulating static electricity). She did. Three times. When he asked her the fourth time, she snapped, "I won't say another word!"

At the end of the term, Louise wanted to take the teachers' examination. Superintendent McMahan said that she needed to finish school first. So did her parents. That fall she enrolled as a senior. In October, Superintendent McMahan began visiting her home. At Thanksgiving they became engaged. For Christmas he gave her a diamond, which she wore only in secret. But love had an outlet. Students talked.[58] "Lou Davis is Professor McMahan's pet," they said.

Brothers Jim and Chad told Louise. They did not know about her engagement to Superintendent McMahan. Student talk did not keep him a bachelor. Neither did it cost him his job. The couple married in August 1892 and escaped to Colorado on their honeymoon.[59]

After six terms in Clyde and the birth of a son Eugene, the McMahans moved to Minneapolis, Minnesota. "Mr. McMahan," as Louise called him thereafter, was superintendent of schools. She, against his will, began offering private piano lessons. He argued that her working would belittle his position as superintendent of schools.[60] Louise handled Mr. McMahan "real gentle." She reminded him of his desire for a homestead in Oklahoma. He planned to try for one during the next opening. She wanted to help make and save money for the venture. Besides, they had a maid to do the housework and care for the baby.

If Mr. McMahan continued to object to her teaching, it was not for long. The news releases of her first recital were so complimentary, he seemed pleased. One said it was "the nicest musical entertainment ever given in the city...." Others were equally glowing.[61]

The McMahans went from Minneapolis to Troy, Kansas. While there, they visited Louise's uncle in Kingfisher, Oklahoma Territory. He had a home-

In keeping with her philosophy, philanthropist and promoter of culture Louise Davis McMahan left a fortune to benefit society. (Courtesy the McMahan Foundation)

stead, plus 480 acres of land and a hotel. That sealed the McMahans' future. Mr. McMahan registered for the opening of the Kiowa-Comanche-Apache reservation. The drawing was scheduled for August 6, 1901, but he did not get land. He decided to go to Lawton anyway and open a law office. He built a house at 716 C Avenue and brought the family to it.[62] Louise opened a studio and continued offering piano lessons. In addition, she supervised her domestic help, participated in several cultural clubs and activities and supported her husband's practice of law.[63]

Among the numerous problems arising in the new land was a shortage of water. Residents had to buy it bucket by bucket, barrel by barrel. On March 4, 1904, a devastating prairie fire threatened to destroy the whole town. Starting in the Wichita Mountains, where farmers were burning grass, it spread with hurricane speed to the edge of the residential district.[64] People fought with wet blankets, sacks, brooms—anything and everything. Wind raged, blowing sand and gravel and cutting the arms and faces of the firefighters. The strength of the wind, however, helped save the city. As houses caught, it blew out the blazes.

The McMahans helped modernize the city and promoted its cultural development. They encouraged Eugene in his school work, providing him with pets in town and in the country. Mr. McMahan bought a relinquished homestead near Geronimo, and the family lived there part-time.[65] Louise dealt kindly with the pets and missed those who died about as much as Eugene did. She even taught one of the dogs to sing while she played the piano. And when her housekeepers were troubled, Louise was there to help.[66]

From the time Eugene was a child, he made his own money and saved some. He sold magazines and newspapers and worked for the Lawton and Oklahoma City newspapers. In 1912, he enrolled in the University of Oklahoma. Louise was very proud and protective of him. She encouraged him in his fraternity activities, but was concerned about his new habit of smoking. He was becoming a first-class debater when World War I fell in on the United States. Eugene enlisted on December 14, 1917.[67] Torn between worry and patriotism, Louise was sick at heart. She wept, prayed, and wrestled with the problem of her only child training for possible death. He became an officer, but "fought the war in Texas." Germany was defeated, so the war was over on November 11, 1918.

While in Texas, Eugene became interested in oil. Both his parents regretted his "gambling" on leases, oil stock, and the like. Eugene prospered a bit, then failed dreadfully. He stuck to the business and rode failure to great success. Eugene opened an office in San Antonio and insisted that his parents join him there. His insistence might have been due to his short and recently failed marriage.[68] The McMahans rented their Oklahoma property to military men and moved their furniture to another home in San Antonio. Mr. McMahan became a silent partner with his son. Louise had time to pursue a second career—painting. She had enjoyed it next to music, but had had no time to paint.

Mr. McMahan's health slowly deteriorated. Louise cared for him at home as long as she could, then hired a night nurse to assist her. They and the doctors could not save him. Neither could they save Eugene a few years later.[69] He developed a malignant lung. Following surgery, he improved, but a blood clot formed and he was gone.

Brokenhearted and alone for the first time in her life, Louise threw herself, her money, and her expertise into building a home for the Foundation in Lawton. By 1948, the Foundation building stood as a classic monument to a husband and son. The first floor served as offices and a cultural center. It had an auditorium, kitchen, and dining room. Louise's paintings decorated the walls. She moved to the second floor.[70] The Foundation became the center for numerous types of meetings and small conferences: the Woman's Forum, music clubs, Great Plains Writers—anything not political or controversial. Among the famous people who appeared there was Eleanor Roosevelt.[71]

Soon after the Foundation was finished and furnished, Louise announced plans to build an auditorium in honor of her husband and son. With the help of the Board of Trustees and others, a beautiful half-million-dollar building was presented to the city of Lawton. It was dedicated on March 11, 1954.[72]

That not being enough, Louise announced to her secretary, Jennie McCutcheon, "I'm going to write a book." From that declaration came *Reminiscences and Scrapbook* in 1957.[73] This indomitable Oklahoma woman had fulfilled a third ambition in addition to her housewifery and motherhood. They were music, art, and writing. But she did them, especially writing, honoring others: her husband, son, friends, relatives, domestic help, and even the family pets.

Louise Davis McMahan died in 1988 at age ninety-two. Her contributions continue to provide assistance for others, and will for generations to come. One of the Foundation's recent projects was the building of the Media Center for the Lawton Public Schools.[74] It is equipped with everything for the promotion of excellence in education, including a broadcasting station.

****

All missionaries were educators, but not all educators were missionaries. It remains the same today. Women did not win the professional status as educators until more recent times. The first "professional" teachers in Indian Territory, both Indian and white, male and female, came from the East. The Five Civilized Tribes and those living in their area had schools soon after their arrival in the 1830s. Those living on the west side got schools after the Civil War. Women were among the teachers. Herein are examples of more recent educators who excelled in that profession.

Chapter 7
EDUCATORS-INNOVATORS

ELEANOR M. WEST JOHNSON
(1892-1987)
"The Nation's Teacher"

Oklahoma can lay claim to "The Nation's Teacher." At least part claim. She was Eleanor (Elnora) West Johnson, founder of *My Weekly Reader* and much more. Read by millions of elementary students around the country, the newspaper's first issue rolled from the American Education Press on September 21, 1928.[1] At that time, according to the book, *Drumright! The Glory Days of a Boomtown*, Eleanor was a teacher and principal at Litchfield, a wing school in the Drumright School System. Believed to have been named for the Litchfield Oil Company, active in the area, the two-room, frame school building stood near Tide Water Refinery south of town.[2]

Eleanor was led to found *My Weekly Reader* because she realized that children needed to know more about people and events in the world. Fortunately, through a friend, she met William Blakey, an owner of American Education Press in Columbus, Ohio. She told him about her dream of a grade school newspaper. He listened with great interest. Sixteen months later, the two met again and formulated her dream into reality.[3]

Eleanor continued teaching and writing. She moved to York, Pennsylvania, for a short time as assistant superintendent of schools, then to Lakewood, Ohio, as superintendent.[4] In 1934, Eleanor joined *Weekly Reader* ("My" had been deleted) full time. Other school publications, such as *Current Events*, sprouted from Eleanor's creation. She developed into an author of textbooks, a lecturer, and a consultant while continuing her duties as a housewife.[5]

Born in the mountains near Jugtown, Pennsylvania, Eleanor came to Oklahoma at the turn of the century with her family. She attended schools and "graduated from Oklahoma College in 1913."[6] (Because many records have vanished, that "college" has not been located by this writer.) Through the early years of Oklahoma, Eleanor taught in Lawton, Chickasha, Oklahoma City, and Drumright. Officials at the latter school provided the following information:[7] "In 1913, Clifford West and his sister, Elnora [*sic*], took over Litchfield. She taught grades 1-3 with 34 pupils, and he taught grades 4-8 with 37 pupils.[8] West resigned in 1925 to become assistant county superintendent of schools. Eleanor replaced him as principal." In 1928 she married Ed Johnson. A year later she became principal at Fairview, also in the Drumright School System.

Meanwhile the lady continued her formal education. She graduated with honors from the University of Chicago, earned a master's degree at Columbia University, and received an honorary doctorate in literature from Hood College. She taught in both schools and the University of Pittsburgh.[9] After retirement, Eleanor served as a consultant for *Weekly Reader*. She was involved in the paper's revival during the 1970s. Her retirement home was Gaithersburg, Maryland.[10]

How did an early-day Oklahoma college graduate and teacher accomplish so much in one short lifetime? How could anybody achieve that much? A copy of the letter she wrote to Janice Skene, the first high school student to receive the Eleanor Johnson Scholarship, might reveal the answer. It said:

Dear Janice,[11]

I want to tell you something important that I have learned from my long life. It is this: Dream big dreams.

When I started out, I was a teacher with a pencil and some ideas—some dreams. Now one of those dreams is *Weekly Reader*—the largest children's newspaper in the world.

The other is Weekly Reader Children's Book Club—the largest hardcover children's book club in the world.

I was lucky, of course, Not all dreams come true. But there are things you can do to help your dreams materialize.

First, know what you want to achieve. Get specific. Write it down and put it where you can see it.

Second, know why you want your dream to come true. Think about your motivations. Know your purposes. Know yourself.

Third, map out a definite plan for achieving

Eleanor M. West Johnson, founder of My Weekly Reader, Current Events, *and other educational publications, was a teacher in four Oklahoma public schools. (Courtesy Weekly Reader)*

your dreams. Start with modest ideas, but don't be afraid. Don't be afraid to plan for bigger and more complex dreams. If you plan for them, they're more than likely to happen.

So, dream big dreams. Then work for the success you dream about.

Good luck,

Eleanor M. Johnson

P.S. I'm still dreaming!!!

Eleanor's advice hinged on her everyday philosophy: "Quality is built on a dream, a practical policy, clear standards and hard work."[12]

Sadness enveloped the American Education Press members and friends when Eleanor West Johnson died that December day in 1987. She was ninety-four years of age.[13]

DR. JEANETTE SMITH CROSBY
(1872-1955)
A Widow Who Beat the Odds

When Jeanette Smith Crosby's husband Edwin died in 1908, she was left in a new land with seven children. The family had been in Western Oklahoma only six months, having moved there for Edwin's health. The move did not help him, and Jeanette wondered if it helped any of them.[14]

Using a cliché common in those days, she did have "an ace in the hole." She had taught school at Little Falls, Minnesota, so she was qualified to work in that field, which was still developing in the area. The state of Oklahoma was only one year old at the time and was struggling to perfect its educational system. Jeanette applied for a position and got one as English teacher at Lawton High School.[15]

Ambitious and eager to increase the family income, the portly woman entered the race for Comanche County Superintendent of Public Instruction. Seven men entered the competition against her.[16] Harold, one of Jeanette's two sons, and Genevieve C. Rehkopf, a daughter, told her story in *Prairie Lore*, an historical magazine of Southwestern Oklahoma. Harold was one of those who went on the campaign trail for his mother. She won.

During Jeanette's two terms in office, she visited every school in the county at least once.[17] In those days, there were no school lunch programs, so on a trip to Fletcher she went to a cafe at noon. The waitress took her order—a steak. Jeanette waited ten, twelve mintues, then asked how much longer she would have to wait. The girl answered, "About fifteen minutes." Not being one to waste time, Jeanette promised to be back and went for a walk.

Below: Dr. Jeanette Smith Crosby had seven children when her husband died in 1908. She reentered the teaching profession, earned a doctor's degree, and became a professor at Southwestern State University at Weatherford while raising her children to be outstanding citizens of Western Oklahoma.

As she returned to the cafe minutes later, she saw the waitress in the butcher shop ordering her steak.[18]

One of Jeanette's most successful programs while in office was the establishment of "Moonlight School" and "Reading Circle" for blacks. She was stopped on many occasions and thanked for giving those people an opportunity to learn.

In 1915 Jeanette joined the faculty of Southwestern State Teachers College at Weatherford where she served in at least three different positions: Associate Professor of Education, Dean of Women, and Head of Tests and Measurements Department.[19] The lady, who wouldn't waste time, took a sabbatical leave in 1924 to earn a master's degree from the University of Oklahoma. At age sixty she took another leave and earned a Ph.D. from the University of California at Berkeley.[20]

Jeanette's success interested Governor Leon Phillips. He appointed her to the State Board of Eleemosynary Schools—those dependent on charity for support. That position was in addition to her responsibilities to her home and children and her position at the college. She was a devout Presbyterian and an enthusiastic Democrat. She was active in Eastern Star, Delta Kappa Gamma (an honorary teachers' organization), and PEO.[21]

What gave this lady on the move such drive? For starters, one of her Smith parents was in the lineage of President James A. Garfield. For another, she was born during the lashing month of March 1872, in Tomah, Wisconsin, a cold area, which requires movement to endure. Of course, those are suppositions, but true.[22]

The Smith family moved to Pipestone, Minnesota, a stimulating area and perhaps a bit mysterious. Blessed with a dull red clay soil base, it was sacred to the Indians—a place to mine stone for their ceremonial pipes. They kept the quarries neutral during wars.[23]

Jeanette graduated from State Normal School at Mankato, Minnesota, and Pillsbury Finishing School at Owatonna. She was teaching when she and Edwin W. Crosby married in 1886. He operated a boot and shoe store.[24] Jeanette continued teaching while bearing seven children: Clifford, Jeanette, Edith, Harold, Alice, and twins Margarete and Mildred. Alice drowned while on a scouting trip at age thirteen.[25] Edwin's physical problems began after he fell from the roof of his home. He had climbed up to smother sparks and repair a flue. He was never well again. Jeanette inspired and aided the Crosby children to get an education. All of them, who lived to adulthood, earned bachelors degrees, and three earned master's degrees.[26]

In 1948 Jeanette retired from Southwestern to live with her daughter and son-in-law, Mr. and Mrs. L.G. Nelson, in Oklahoma City. She died in 1955 and was buried in Weatherford Cemetery. The family established a revolving memorial fund at Southwestern, and it grew into a sizable amount.

LUCILLE TAYLOR PINTZ
(1913-   )
Progenitor of Head Start

For the past two centuries, millions of footsteps have led to Oklahoma. In like manner, many have led out. A very important set leading out in the mid-1900s was that of Lucille Taylor Pintz, a Sulphur native and graduate of the local schools. The progenitor of Head Start, Pintz received the Nation's Meritorious Award.[27]

The program began at the University of Chicago in 1962 after President John F. Kennedy invited two hundred members of the American Home Economics Association to meet and formulate plans for improving the welfare of the American people. Lucille was one of them. Since 1945, she had been associated with the Bureau of Indian Affairs at Fort Apache Indian Reservation and the public schools of White River, Arizona. As teacher and agricultural extension supervisor of the Phoenix area, she had lots of ideas. One was to determine the cause of multiple school dropouts, especially among minorities. Another was to develop possible solutions.[28]

Although some parents on the reservation worked at the Indian Agency and the Forestry Service, most depended on small incomes from cattle. They lived in wickiups made from coarse bear grass pulled from the earth in clumps. They spoke their native language; thus their children knew very few words of English. In addition, many were malnourished and had never been off the reservation. As a result, they fell behind in school, became discouraged, and quit.[29]

Lucille thought it would be advantageous for the very young to have a program like kindergarten. They could learn English, be taught the importance of good hygiene, and receive proper health care. Those things, plus wholesome nutrition, would prepare them for coping with school and later life.[30]

Lucille Taylor Pintz, progenitor of Head Start, shows two of her numerous awards. (Taken by the author)

When Lucille presented her idea, she called it "Early Start." The committee and general assembly at Chicago approved it, then sent it to President Kennedy. He and his commission, headed by Sargent Shriver, liked the idea, but Shriver wanted to change the name to "Head Start." Lucille agreed, then recommended Dr. Sue Sadow to write the program.[31]

After Lyndon B. Johnson became president, Dr. Florence Lowe, a Texan who attended the Chicago meeting, prevailed upon him to continue the program. He got it funded, and in 1963 and it began spreading. Today, it reaches throughout the country. Parents are encouraged to participate and to support their children. Besides training in English, youngsters receive good nutrition, proper health care, and stimulating social interaction.[32] Due to Head Start, more students have finished high school, gone on to college, and become leaders in their communities.

Prior to her work with Indians, Lucille made footprints in another field. In 1942, she became a home economics teacher in a Japanese relocation center. Later she was a relocation advisor and administrator.[33] The camp was on a Pima Indian reservation in the middle of the Arizona desert where there was nothing except sand until the army barracks were constructed. The Japanese came from confinement in horse stables at Delmar, California.[34]

There were 20,000 men, women, and children in two camps, Rivers and Canal, seven miles apart. Some were born in America and Hawaii (Hawaii was not a state at that time), while others were natives of Japan in this country illegally.[35] The school had education classes for adults as well as for children. They were especially interested in United States history. And being expert gardeners, they landscaped the area with native shrubs thanks to water brought from a reservoir in the mountains. They even grew roses and chrysanthemums.[36]

Among Lucille's students was Daniel Inouye, today (1991) a United States Senator from Hawaii. Other members of his family, also, were there. Inouye was among the resentful students who pounded on the desks and demanded to know: "Is this really American Democracy?"

Pintz replied: "This is war!"[37]

Inouye and several other Japanese youths, who no longer seemed a threat to America, were allowed to volunteer for military service. Their story of heroism on the battlefield has been recognized for many years. It was there Inouye lost an arm, for which he received the Purple Heart. Some young Japanese-Americans were allowed to attend college.[38]

In 1943, Eleanor Roosevelt and then Secretary of War Henry L. Stimson visited the camp and were impressed by the efficiency of its operation. Columnist Westbrook Pegler blasted the United States authorities for having imprisoned the Japanese.

Below: Third from right, second row, is Lucille Taylor Pintz with some of her students at a Japanese relocation center in Arizona during World War II. One of her students was future U.S. Senator Daniel Inouye of Hawaii. (Courtesy Lucille Taylor Pintz)

A teacher in an Indian school for several years after World War II, Lucille Taylor Pintz held seminars in various places. Here she is at right, back row. (Courtesy Lucille Taylor Pintz)

When their mother country surrendered, they were released. That was when Lucille transferred to the Indian Service.

Lucille received numerous honors and awards for service to education. Not only that, but she met her husband Bob Pintz from Wisconsin at camp. He was in charge of internal security. The army patrolled outside the camp.[39]

A graduate of Oklahoma State University and Colorado State, Lucille did postgraduate study at the University of Chicago. She taught home economics in Ardmore before entering service for the War Department and the Department of Interior. She has traveled in all fifty states except Maine, in the Scandinavian countries, and in India, China, and Africa.[40] After spending forty-six years in Arizona and losing her husband, Lucille's footprints led back home to Sulphur, Oklahoma, in 1988. She is currently (1993) in Arizona.

ANABEL FLEMING (THOMASON), ESQ.
(1874-1949)
First Woman Lawyer in Indian Territory

Credited as being the first woman lawyer west of the Mississippi River, which might not be true, Anabel Fleming was honored nationwide when Judge Hosea Townsend issued her a license to practice law in Federal Court. The presentation was made in 1899 in Pauls Valley, Indian Territory.[41]

Articles about her appeared in local, national, and international publications such as *Harper's Bazaar*, *St. Louis Post Dispatch*, *St. Louis Republic*, *Dallas Morning News*, *New York Times*, and the *London Times*.... But this petite young woman with smiling brown eyes did not allow her instant fame to swell her ego.

She went back to work in the newly established Federal Court in Pauls Valley. Anabel centered her attention on the docket at hand. She attested to cases ranging from the simplest to the most serious: execution.[42] Now how could a woman on the frontier have the background or influence to become a certified lawyer-judge? Surely, she did not have that much mettle. Or did she?

The offshoot of American-Scotch pioneers, Anabel was born a sturdy and determined Texan at Clarksville. Her earlier ancestors in Delaware were Revolutionary soldiers, branded "Blue Hen's Chickens."[43] The title originated during the War for American Independence when Captain Caldwell

Below: Anabel Fleming (Thomason), Esquire, was not only a lawyer but also a federal judge. She received a license to practice law in 1899. (Courtesy Oklahoma Historical Society)

said: "to be unconquerable, a game cock has to be 'a blue hen's chicken'." His regiment became known by that title. So did the state of Delaware and its people.[44]

Anabel was the oldest daughter of nine children born to James Titus and Martha Childers Fleming. James Fleming was an attorney and rancher whose land had finally been claimed by drought. He moved to the city.[45] Anabel attended private schools in Texas and graduated from Kidd-Key College in Sherman. Throughout her youth, she was "her father's daughter." She accompanied and helped him throughout his legal and political career.[46]

In 1886 Judge Fleming brought his family to Ardmore, Indian Territory. At that time, Ardmore was only a village growing out of the 700 Ranch. A railroad was coming through from Texas to Kansas.[47] Mrs. Fleming set an example for the children and all the young people in the community. She organized the first subscription school and became active in the Methodist Church. In addition, she participated in women's clubs, common to that era.

The family lived in Ardmore nine years when Mr. Fleming took a job with the Federal Court in Pauls Valley and moved the family there. Anabel, now twenty-one years old, helped her father get organized, then became an apprentice in his office. Pauls Valley was on the same railroad as Ardmore. Built on the bank of the Washita River, it was surrounded by rich land, producing cotton, grain, alfalfa, and pecans.[48]

Dedicated to the work at hand, Anabel was said to know more law at that time than most of the practicing attorneys. That was before she passed the bar exam.[49] Among the other lawyers in Pauls Valley was Charles H. Thomason from Tennessee. As was fated, the "twain" did meet. Anabel and Charles fell in love and married. That was in 1901. They bought land from Sippia Paul Hull (also featured in this book) and built a house. As was the case in many such transactions during those days, the Thomasons had to reestablish the title to their land after Statehood.[50]

Judge Anabel Fleming Thomason plunged into the duties of housewifery as she had done into Federal Court dockets. She bore four children and became a leader in club, church, and school work. She studied art, painted, and wrote poetry. Her poems appeared in many publications.[51] Descendants of this dedicated woman became legislators, governors and other highly respectable personages.

Her enormously successful life ended at the family home in 1949.[52]

JANE ANNE JAYROE
(1946-)
Miss America, TV Anchorwoman, Scholar

Jane Anne Jayroe put Laverne, Oklahoma, on the map in bigger letters than those generated in newspapers by all the tornadoes which razed the town. And she put it there with more permanence. Further, she brought more credit to Oklahoma than cyclones and continues to do so.[53]

As Miss Oklahoma in 1967, Jane brightened the initial scenes of the Miss America Pageant in Atlantic City, New Jersey. When near the end of the program she took the baton from the maestro's hand and directed the orchestra, she electrified the scene.[54] Without missing a beat or disturbing the musicians, she continued to direct a flawless performance. Her control was as calm and correct as if she had rehearsed the act many times.

Then came the finale. Five of America's most beautiful and talented young women in elegant gowns stood before Master of Ceremonies Bert Parks, the audience and the TV world to hear the judges' decision. "Second runner-up..., First runner-up...." It was not necessary for Bert Parks to say any more. Everybody knew that Miss Oklahoma was Miss America![55] Unknown to Jane and that rousing, cheering multitude around her, the TV audience in Laverne and all of Oklahoma also was shouting with pride and excitement. It was as if they all had won the crown.

Jane, as Miss America, was on a detour from the road she had followed since birth near the border of Oklahoma's Panhandle. With a jet plane and automobiles at her disposal, she rushed from place to place speaking, signing autographs for admirers, leading parades—while traveling 200,000 miles. That is equivalent to eight trips around the world.[56]

All the while, Jane was bringing more distinction to Laverne, the state of Oklahoma, and America. Her proudest accomplishment that year, she said, "was the two weeks she entertained troops in Viet Nam."[57] As a USO entertainer, Jane was the first Miss America to visit a combat zone during wartime. After that it became a tradition for Miss Americas.[58]

When Jane's year of detour ended, she returned to Oklahoma City University where she completed

Miss America, 1968, Jane Anne Jayroe has served the people of Oklahoma in several capacities: as a TV anchorwoman, a lecturer, a health reporter, and, greatest of all, an inspiration. (Courtesy KOCO-TV, Oklahoma City)

a bachelor of arts degree in Vocal Music Education. From there her road led to the University of Tulsa for a master's degree and marriage to an attorney.[59] Jane worked for the Oklahoma Department of Education and the Oklahoma Educational Television Authority and with Art Linkletter co-hosted a syndicated series on "The Other School System."

Education was a priority in Jane's life, but again she detoured.[60] In 1978 she became news anchor for KOCO-TV in Oklahoma City, then transferred to a similar position at KSAS-TV, a Dallas-Fort Worth station. Oklahoma won her back in 1984. She spent three years in Oklahoma City at KTVY-TV before transferring back to KOCO-TV. At both stations she was news anchor and a producer of special programs.

Before her fans realized it, Jane was back in education as a candidate for a doctor's degree in Communications at Oklahoma University. That did not exempt her from her constant involvement in public service. She sat on committees, lectured, entertained, judged contests, and served in her church as a Bible teacher and choir member. All that and more did not make her immune from the duties of raising her son, Tyler Jayroe Peterson, and visiting her parents in Laverne.[61]

Jane was born at Clinton to Pete and Helene Jayroe and became the sister of little Judy Jayroe. At that time the family lived in Hammon where Mr. Jayroe was a teacher in the public schools. As Jane grew up, her parents lived and taught in other Western Oklahoma communities.[62] They taught and encouraged their girls to get an education, gave them special music lessons, and planted in them the ideals of Christianity.

At a very early age Jane began singing in the Methodist Church. In school she took music lessons and participated in special programs. It was there she learned to lead and direct activities. It was there, too, no doubt, she gained the courage which came to the forefront at the Miss America Pageant, prompting her to take the baton and direct the orchestra.[63] Jane's talents and drive included sports. She played basketball and was on the team when Laverne reached second place in the state play-off. She carried both sports and music into Oklahoma City University—studying, playing, directing, and producing plays.

Among Jane's numerous honors as a student and on the job were Miss Laverne, Miss Cinderella, Miss All-College Queen, Outstanding News Personality, as well as recipient of the Muscular Dystrophy Broadcast Journalism Award, and the Scripps Howard and the Gabriel awards.[64] She was honored by the YMCA, the OSU College of Home Economics, the Adolescent Task Force, and schools throughout the state for her support of education. More recently she was named Outstanding Woman in Oklahoma by the Town Club Business and Professional Women.[65]

Jane has been featured in numerous publications and will surely be featured in many others as she proceeds in her current position at the Oklahoma Health Sciences Center in Oklahoma City. Her broadcasts on health are as popular, and even more profitable than were her prior reports on news.[66]

****

Oklahoma has been honored with two other Miss Americas—Norma Smallwood in 1926 and Susan Powell in 1981. In 1959 Anita Bryant was second runner-up.[67] Norma was a native of Bristow. She entered the contest as Miss Tulsa. She married George Bruce, president of an oil company, and moved to Kansas, where she died in 1966. Susan was from Elk City and was a music student at Oklahoma City University. She married David Parsons and moved to New York where she became a member of the New York City Opera Company.[68] Anita, a native of Barnsdall, became a popular entertainer, but encountered a few "plagues" along the way. Her last known home was in Atlanta, Georgia. She now entertains at the Anita Bryant Theater in Eureka Springs, Arkansas.[69]

As some of the Oklahoma Miss Americas left the state, two moved in. They were Donna Axum Whitworth and Cheryl Prewitt Salem. Donna, who received her crown as Miss Arkansas, settled with her husband at Bartlesville. Cheryl, who won as Miss Mississippi, moved to Tulsa. Both ladies are active in communications, and Cheryl also operates her own clothing store.[70]

****

Education led to legalized military service for women in World War II, but they had been active and even leaders in battles for eons. In the Bible, Deborah led an attack against the Canaanites in 1316 B.C. Ages later Joan of Arc led the French to success and failure. In America an Indian princess, Mollie Colbert, led some Chickasaw women in the Battle of New Orleans. They helped their husbands who were fighting under Andrew Jackson.[71] Mollie became the grandmother of Cyrus Harris, first governor (chief) of the Chickasaws, after the tribe came west. Hundreds of thousands of women have served in the military since 1940. Four Oklahomans are recognized herein for their valor.

1

Chapter 8
MILITARY PERSONNEL

IRENE STURM LEFEBVRE
A Witness to Victory

It was a long, dangerous hop from the safety and fields of sweet-smelling wheat in northern Oklahoma to the acrid "hell on earth" stench of World War II in the South Pacific, but Irene Sturm Lefebvre made it and lived to reminisce about it.[1] As a member of the Women's Army Corps, better known as WACS, Irene was attached to the Top Secret Command of General Douglas MacArthur as he "island hopped" to keep his vow, "I shall return." He made that vow after President Franklin Roosevelt ordered him to leave the Philippines and take command in Australia.[2] General Jonathan Wainwright was left in charge of American forces, who were soon overrun by Japanese and forced to surrender. This grieved MacArthur, making him more determined to retake the country.[3]

Irene and her group arrived in nearby New Guinea via ship in October 1944, the same month MacArthur's forces came ashore on Leyte in the Philippine Islands. They settled on a hill at Hollandia where engineers had prepared roads, bridges, and quarters of concrete footings and burlap walls. Each hut served six girls. Their food was regular dehydrated G.I. rations with an occasional treat of eggs.[4]

Almost completely confined to quarters, the girls went about their respective jobs without weapons. Irene was a secretary for the Radar and Countermeasures of Combat Forces. When it was necessary for her or any of the other girls to go out, armed guards accompanied them.

"Natives were very curious about us," Irene said. "The men and boys were naked until the United States provided them with G.I. uniforms. The women and girls wore skirts only."[5] Dark-skinned, the natives had black, wooly hair and wore a variety of personal attachments, ranging from sticks to bones. Those in the highlands lived in grass huts, while those in the swamps had small houses on stilts which protected them from animals and floods from torrential rainfall. The climate of New Guinea is said to be the "worst in the world." The principal food of the natives was sweet potatoes, taro roots, bananas, and pigs.[6]

Six weeks after Irene landed in New Guinea, her unit "hopped" to Leyte in the Philippines. Their first station was Tacloban, then Tolos.[7] General MacArthur kept his vow to "return" when his forces assaulted the enemy on Mindoro, Philippines, on December 15, 1944. Allied infantry and armored "Alligators," already on land, joined forces with the fleets of admirals Thomas C. Kinkaid and William Halsey to double the attack on the enemy. The naval battles proved catastrophic to the Japanese fleet.[8]

Manila was the next destination and the last for Irene. The city had been almost completely destroyed, but the WACS' quarters were a bit improved from those on New Guinea. They lived in a boys' school until the end of the war. That came on August 10, 1945, almost immediately after the atomic bombs obliterated most of Hiroshima and Nagasaki, Japan.[9] The end brought freedom to the prisoners of war and great rejoicing to the Allied world. Irene witnessed the wild celebration in Manila. Despite years of devastation and deprivation, the city sprang to life with spectacular fireworks.[10] Irene sailed for home and was discharged

Below: Following military service in World War II, Irene Sturm Lefebvre raised a family, then became a writer, including the book, Cherokee Strip in Transition. *She is shown here during World War II. (Courtesy Paul Lefebvre)*

on October 30, 1945, with the rank of Technician Third Grade.[11]

Was she often in danger like the men? Irene seemed surprised at the question. "Oh, yes. We women hit the foxholes sometimes, same as the men."

What prompted her to go into military service? "I was the oldest of six children," she answered, "and had a natural tendency for patriotism. I felt I needed to do my part for my country."[12]

Irene's heritage was a natural for patriotism. A native of Medford, Oklahoma, she is the daughter of Loyde P. and Merle Irene Sturm, pioneers of Grant County. Mrs. Sturm was born there in a sod house. After graduating from public schools, Irene completed studies at Enid Business College in 1938. She was a legal secretary in Medford before entering military service. Following her discharge, she became a legal secretary in Oklahoma City.[13]

Irene married Paul E. Lefebvre, a commercial artist, and the couple established a home in Oklahoma City. She became her husband's secretary and researcher. The two collaborated on a column—"It's a-Happening Everywhere—Driving in Oklahoma"—and on brochures for various chambers of commerce, as well as for other publications.[14] From that came her own writings, primarily for the *Daily Oklahoman*'s magazine section, "Orbit." As a charter member and windjammer (newsletter editor) of the Women's Posse of the Westerners, Irene edited the organization's *Brand Book*. She has recently completed two volumes of *Cherokee Strip in Transition*, commissioned by the city of Enid.[15] Those volumes are in three different bindings: paper, cloth and leather.[16]

Irene has received numerous awards for her writing. She has been active in civic work as host for international visitors for the Oklahoma City Chamber of Commerce, was a Girl Scout leader, and a member of the Obedience Training Class for her son's dog, Beowulf.[17] All of these activities and more were performed in conjunction with housewifery and bearing three children. They include Michelle, wife of Joseph Carter and publisher of the *Times Herald* at the Port of Catoosa, Oklahoma; he is director of the Will Rogers Memorial in Claremore. Paul Lefebvre II is vice president of Southwest Bank, Oklahoma City. His wife Pat is self-employed in the computer business and cares for the couple's son John Paul. He is a second grader at Washington Irving school in Edmond.[18]

Mark Lefebvre, the youngest, is a part-time student and business manager for the family's studio, Lefebvre Imagineering.

And what else would Irene Sturm Lefebvre like to do? "Return to the battlefields of New Guinea and the Philippines, someday, to see what influence, if any, Americans left there during World War II."[19]

MAJ. JOHNNIE LEE PENNINGTON
Made Footprints Around the World

Teacher, WAF, humanitarian and holder of enough commendations, awards, and photographs to decorate a house—that is the micro-record of Johnnie Lee Pennington, Major, USAF, Ret. But there is much more. As a native of Southern Oklahoma and the daughter of a teacher, Ila Pennington, Johnnie Lee started her education at Drake, a two-room, country school in the southern part of Murray County. It is now a ghost town.[20]

Johnnie Lee transferred to Sulphur and, during her high school years, worked at Richards' Five and Dime Store and at Belleview Plunge, a popular local swimming pool. At the latter, she was a basket checker and swimming instructor. She also worked as a counselor in a youth camp at Fort Worth, Texas.

Johnnie Lee attended East Central State College (now University) at Ada, but graduated with a B.S. degree from the University of Oklahoma in 1953. Her majors were Home Economics and Physical Education. Immediately, she entered the teaching profession in Isabel, Kansas, later going to Pratt, Kansas. Her subjects were predominantly in her major fields. In addition, she served as girls' basketball coach and Pep Club sponsor.[21]

Earlier in her life, Johnnie Lee had been smitten with a desire to serve in a broader sense, so she entered the United States Air Force in 1965. She began Officers Training School at Lackland Air Force Base, San Antonio, Texas. From there she went to Amarillo Air Force Base for a training course and graduated with the highest average. After receiving her regular officer's commission, Johnnie Lee became chief of supply operations at Korat Royal Air Force Base, Korat, Thailand, and was there during the Tet Offensive. Her commendations and advances in rank continued throughout her military career.[22]

Johnnie Lee recalled many memories of exotic Thailand (old Siam): "If the natives like you," she

Major Johnnie Lee Pennington receiving a decoration in 1985 from the Assistant Deputy in Charge of Staff, Logistics Headquarters, Strategic Air Command, Omaha, Nebraska. (Courtesy Johnnie Lee Pennington)

said, "they are okay. But if not, they can be vicious. There was so much poverty. A father could feed his family on twenty-five cents a day." The female servants were called "hooch girls." Most of them never saw an ironing board. "They spread a blanket on the floor," Johnnie Lee said, "and got down over it to do their ironing. They all liked to work for the Americans, because they could make more money."[23]

After becoming a captain, Johnnie Lee went to Korea and Viet Nam on short assignments. At one base, the only other women were "mamasans" (cleaning women) and Red Cross workers. One of the "mamasans" was impressed by Johnnie Lee—her size, uniform and captain's bars. She touched them with the speed and delicacy of a butterfly.[24] "Number one," she said in her native language and smiled.

There was danger in Viet Nam of being so near the front line, but in certain situations Johnnie Lee could defend herself. "I had to qualify well enough to receive the Small Arms Expert Marksmanship Ribbon."

Johnnie Lee enjoyed her stay in the Far East, but she was happy to get home. "If I hadn't been in uniform," she said, "I could have kissed the tarmac [asphalt runway]."[25] The major served and studied in several United States military installations, including Hawaii and Florida. She was in Florida when Hurricane Camille struck with such great

devastation. It was there, however, that she received two master's degrees from the Florida Institute of Technology at Melbourne. One was in Logistics Management, the other in Business Management.[26] While in service, she also chalked up 650 classroom hours from various military schools.

Her European tour of duty (1980-1983) was as Chief, Supply Readiness, under the Headquarters USAFE Assistant for Readiness until the Directorate was abolished during reorganization. During that time, Johnnie Lee visited many countries from Norway in the "Land of the Midnight Sun" to Egypt, land of pyramids, white hot skies, and searing deserts.[27]

Early in Johnnie Lee's career, news of her accomplishments reached into the civilian sector. Leaders of Women's Organization, Chicago, listed her as one of the "Outstanding Young Women of America."

Because of her mother's ill health, Johnnie Lee retired in 1985 and returned to Sulphur. Since then, she has devoted herself to volunteer and humanitarian work, concentrating on American Legion activities. She began as a member of the Veterans' Day Committee, then became chairman in 1988. The outstanding parade that year had between 150 and 200 entries.[28] Some of Johnnie Lee's other services were as Adjutant for Platt National Park Post 148, Sulphur; District 5B First Vice-Commander; Assistant on Finance Programs and Youth Activities; Coordinator of and Contributor to Needy Programs; Judge Advocate; Oklahoma Department Historian; and Reporter on Tourism to the local Chamber of Commerce. She also reinstituted awards for the outstanding senior boy and girl at Sulphur High School and at Oklahoma School for the Deaf.[29]

Johnnie Lee's membership reaches to the Calvary Baptist Church, the Air Force Association, the Retired Officers Association, and the Society of Logistics Engineers. She is active in all of them.

She has no regrets at having followed the path she chose. "I did my bit for youth," she said, "I did my bit for democracy, and now I'm doing my bit for the community, which did so much for me."[30]

MAJ. HELEN FREUDENBERGER HOLMES
(1915-   )
Lady on the Wing

Helen Freudenberger did it all. After graduating from Coyle High School as valedictorian in

War and illness did not stop Major Helen Freudenberger Holmes. She forged ahead to become a homemaker, mayor of Guthrie, author, and more. This photograph was taken in Heidelberg, Germany, in 1947. (Courtesy Helen Freudenberger Holmes)

1932 and Oklahoma A&M College at Stillwater with honors in 1936, this flying lady took off into professions unlimited.[31]

Her first position was editor of the *Maud Daily Enterprise*, and next she became public relations director back at A&M. The later position included writing material for state and national publications, such as *Life*. In addition, she appeared three times a week on radio from a Tulsa station. Helen went from there to instructor in journalism and organized Theta Sigma Phi on campus.[32]

Meanwhile, this "Lady on Wings" earned a master's degree from the University of Wisconsin at Madison. Remaining on top of her work, she was a University Scholar. Then world affairs changed her direction.[33] In 1942, it looked as if the Allies were losing World War II. The Japanese were blasting through the Far East—Malaya, Singapore, Burma.... The Fascists of Germany and Italy were rolling over the rest of Europe and the Soviet Union as if they were paper empires.[34]

The United States was sorely threatened. Its citizens were fired to patriotic hostility. The younger generation, not already drafted, volunteered for the military services. Helen Freudenberger was one of them. She went on military leave from the college to become the first member of the Women's Army Auxiliary Corps (WAACS) from Oklahoma in the first class of officer candidates in that organization. Helen received a commission as Second Lieutenant and became a public relations officer in charge of the *Minority Press* at Fort Des Moines, Iowa.[35]

From there she transferred to the Military District of Washington to be in charge of public relations for the WAACS at that place. The WAAC was integrated into the Army in 1943 as the Women's Army Corps (WACS). This change moved Helen into the position of intelligence officer with the Army Air Corps in Washington, D.C. After VE Day, she went to Germany with the Army of Occupation as an intelligence officer. Later she became assistant to the Inspector General of the Stuttgart Military Command.

An illness sent her into retirement as a major and to treatment in Veterans Administration facilities in the United States.[36] After recovery, that "Lady on the Wing" flew in a completely different direction. On December 19, 1949, she married Robert Holmes in Guthrie. They settled on a farm near Coyle, a small town in Logan County. The couple became parents of three children: Charles Matthew, William James, and Andrea Margaret. While they were growing up, Helen participated in all their school activities: the Parent-Teachers' Association, 4-H Club, sports.... When the need arose, she served in several positions as an officer.[37] As a result of her interest and involvement in the school, Helen was chosen Honorary Chapter Farmer of the Coyle Future Farmers of America.

In 1962, death claimed Robert Holmes. His family remained on the farm ten more years, then moved to Guthrie. The children being mature, the "Lady with Wings" flew in a fourth direction. She became a docent for the Oklahoma Territorial Museum in Guthrie and active in Extension Homemakers. She edited and was principal author of the two volumes of *Logan County History*, published in 1979 and 1981. Another of her projects was a book on Guthrie homes.[38]

During those years of history writing, Helen

was making history in politics. She became a member of the City Council, then mayor of Guthrie from 1979 to 1981. At the end of her term, she was far from retiring. She became chairman of several Logan County organizations: the Council on Aging, Friends of the Library, Logan County League of Democrats, and Oklahoma Territory Museum docents.[39]

Each April for about seven years, Helen wrote the "Historical Section" for the *Guthrie Daily Leader's 89er Edition*. She served as coordinator for citizens' participation in the 1989 Centennial Celebration of Oklahoma's first land run.

As a member of Zion Lutheran Church in Guthrie, Helen has been president of its Women's Missionary League and teacher of the Adult Bible Class. Added to all that and more, Helen has spoken on a variety of subjects for organizations and at public gatherings.

Her life on wings reaches back to her parents—German immigrants, John Andrew and Theresa Karmer Freudenberger. Her father was a Spanish-American War veteran and her mother an industrious and inspiring Frau.[40] The eighth and youngest child of the Freudenberger family, Helen grew up on the farm at Coyle. She learned to work and achieve. That was the way she chalked up so many "firsts" in numerous fields of endeavor.

NELLIE BELLE BLACKARD HORSMAN
Military Wives Also Pay Price of Wars

Still not recognized in the lineups of heroes are the millions of military wives who face sacrifice and hardship to follow their men during war or peace. There are constant transfers, usually with children; inadequate housing; a scarcity of food; prejudices against the military.... One of Sulphur's women who traveled the trail is Nellie Belle Blackard Horsman. Married to George Leslie Horsman, she moved fifty times.[41]

Her trek began about 1937 when her husband, whom she affectionately calls "Pappy," was a lieutenant in the CCCs. He was assigned to Grand Junction, Colorado, where the couple found a small apartment at an inflated rate of rent. About a year later, Pappy was transferred to Durango, Colorado. The couple lived in one room before locating a small apartment. It was there son George Leslie was born.[42] Pappy's next move was to Baggs, Wyoming, an abandoned fort. The Horsmans' quarters were a wheelwright shop in the rear of a stage

Holding her painting of Mount McKinley, Alaska, Nellie Belle Blackard Horsman sits in her home at Sulphur. She spent years as an army wife, mother, and teacher. (Taken by the Author)

station. That was the birthplace of daughter Madelyn. Since it was more than seventy miles to the nearest hospital, Nellie Belle's attendant was a contract physician with the CCC camp.[43]

When World War II exploded in Europe in 1939, the United States organized an armored force of two divisions, pulling officers with calvalry experience from all over the country. Because of his training at New Mexico Military Institute, Pappy fit that need. "But how they ever found him in Baggs, Wyoming," Nellie Belle quipped, "I'll never know."

In 1940 he was sent to Fort Benning, Georgia. Nellie Belle remained in Baggs to sell their furniture, pack, and drive with two small children in a loaded car to grandparents Blackard and Horsman in Sulphur. It was six weeks before Pappy found housing. Many people would not rent to families with children, while some had signs on their lawns: "G.I.s and dogs not allowed."[44] The family's first home was far out in the piney woods and without heat. Their next was a "shotgun" house in Columbus. It had a fireplace. After Pappy became adjutant of the 82nd Battalion, the Horsmans got quarters on the post.[45]

Nellie Belle's mother came for a visit and had just left on the bus when the Japanese attacked Pearl Harbor. Mr. Blackard's brother Willard was a radio operator on the battleship *Oklahoma*, which was

Seated in front of the mansion they occupied in Japan, the Horsman family includes, left to right: Madelyn, Nellie Belle, Colonel Leslie Horsman, and George Leslie. Standing behind are members of their Japanese household. (Courtesy Nellie Belle Blackard Horsman)

sunk. The families faced anxious hours and news of possible disaster until they traced Mrs. Blackard to Lebanon, Tennessee; from her they learned that Willard had jumped from the *Oklahoma* into flaming waters, but had survived.[46]

Pappy went next to Fort Bragg, North Carolina, where the battalion commandeered a hotel. Nellie Belle closed quarters at Fort Benning, paid bills and followed with the children and baggage. In 1943 the men were assigned to duty in North Africa. Mrs. Blackard and Mrs. Horsman came to Fort Bragg to say goodbye to Pappy. They were barred from going to Fort Dix, New Jersey, the port of embarkation.[47]

After the men left, the women had to do all the necessary duties of moving, generally back to their parents' homes. Nellie Belle led a caravan of five loaded cars heading west of the Mississippi River. At Lebanon, Tennessee, the roads were blocked by an army on maneuvers. The women could find no vacant rooms, so they went to the highway patrol to see if there were some way out of town.[48] "Lady!" a patrolman bristled at Nellie Belle, "don't you know there is a war on?"

"We have just sent our husbands off to battle," Nellie Belle bristled back. "Now what are you doing here in the middle of Tennessee?"

The man wanted to put her in jail until his superior officer told him, "You asked for that."[49]

The managers of a hotel came to the women's aid, surrendering their own two rooms. They put in cots and pallets and provided food until the women and children could leave. Nellie Belle and her children returned to Sulphur. She taught at the Deaf School, where she had been employed before she married.[50]

When Pappy earned enough points overseas, he returned to Fort Knox, Kentucky, as a teacher for the army. Nellie Belle left the children in Sulphur with Mrs. Blackard and joined him. She got a job teaching Latin, Spanish and English. When the war ended in 1945, Pappy went to Fort Chaffee, Arkansas, to process men coming home from Europe. Nellie Belle drove to Sulphur alone, got the children, and took them to relatives at Muldrow, Oklahoma, near Fort Chaffee. Madelyn's first-year school was in a log cabin, while George Leslie was already in third grade. Nellie Belle taught in Fort Smith, where she contracted mumps.[51]

Pappy's next station was Fort Lewis, Washington, another processing station, but for men coming home from the Far East. The movers from Fort Chaffee took fifty phonograph records from their packages and stored them in the washing machine. Upon arrival at Fort Lewis, all were broken. During the family's interlude there, the children attended county schools, and Nellie Belle, under contract, served as substitute teacher.[52]

Continuing his career in the army, Pappy transferred to the Intelligence School near Baltimore, Maryland. Nellie Belle drove to Sulphur, left the children with Mrs. Blackard, and went alone to Baltimore. She taught in the county schools until Pappy left for Japan in 1948. Nellie Belle went to Sulphur after the children and drove to Seattle.[53] The three flew to Japan, but the car went by boat. Their quarters were in a commandeered hotel, and food was scarce. They had soup, made with peanut butter, bacon, and water. No milk was available except for babies under a year old, and Americans were forbidden to eat locally grown food.[54]

In Kobe, the Horsmans lived in a sumptuous, thirty-eight-room mansion belonging to a billionaire and had several servants. The landlady lived in the servants' quarters of eighteen rooms. The surrender of such homes was part of Japan's reparation for losing the war. Pappy went to Korea for fourteen months but Nellie Belle kept the house, taught in the post school, and studied ancient Japanese art, which had almost been lost in that country. Natives now prefer Western art.

After five years in Japan, Pappy returned to the Intelligence School near Baltimore, then transferred to Alaska. For once, the family traveled to Seattle together and took a boat to their destination. They got quarters at Fort Richardson near Anchorage.[55] Nellie Belle began teaching in a Quonset hut where it got so cold that water pipes sometimes froze, and school had to be dismissed. At the completion of a new building she became principal. Occasionally, a bear or moose ventured into the yard, and the children wanted to go pet it. Of course, the animal was driven away immediately.[56]

High school students went by bus to Anchorage. George Leslie and Madelyn graduated there and were attending Oklahoma University when Pappy, then a colonel, retired in 1958. The couple returned to Sulphur. Since then, Nellie Belle has lost Pappy to illness and Lieutenant George Leslie to the war in Viet Nam.

Her musings about military life:[57] She liked Alaska, but Japan was the best place to live, Wyoming the worst. The hardest thing with which to deal was people who tried to "rip-off" military personnel. Maryland had the best school system, but Alaska strove to keep students six months ahead of those in the forty-eight states; they usually lost that much time in transfer.[58]

****

Of all people who need to temper conflict, labor, and sadness with entertainment, it is women. Many have done and still do that. They sing, play games, and tell stories to their sick, restless, and unhappy children. They have to entertain their husbands and others as well.

In the old days unnamed maidens became members of harems to sing and dance for rich and famous masters. Two maidens fortunate enough to be named in the Bible were Miriam, sister of Moses, and Salome, stepdaughter of Herod. Miriam and her maidens performed with songs and timbrels in exultation after the Israelites successfully crossed the Sea of Reeds. Salome danced to please the king in order to win the head of John the Baptist on a platter.[59]

Almost two millenniums later in Indian Territory, parents were, what one might say, the television. They were skilled at entertaining by telling stories of battles and old times. In a distinctly different culture today, entertainers herein reached the zenith of their professions with civility, honor, and remuneration.

of Science and Arts of Oklahoma) at Chickasha, Te Ata developed a program which she performed for the school and public. The presentation included native stories, songs, and dances.[31] She became the first Indian to graduate from Oklahoma College for Women.

To polish her performance, Te Ata attended the Theater School of Carnegie Technology at Pittsburgh, Pennsylvania. Next she braved the wilds and wonders of New York City to satisfy a dream. Her first job was on the stage.[32] She performed in Shakespearean and Greek dramas. One of her roles was that of Andromache in *The Trojan Woman*. Such roles, however, were unrelated to her soul. She wanted to acquaint the public with her own culture. That decreed she develop another program of songs, poems, and dances around her past and her people.[33]

Once completed, Te Ata began entertaining at women's clubs in New York City. Eleanor Roosevelt was a guest at one of her performances and was captivated. When King George VI and Queen Elizabeth visited the Roosevelts at Hyde Park, Eleanor called Te Ata to perform. The royal couple were so impressed, Eleanor called Te Ata to the White House on other occasions. Such approval secured the folklorist's future and guided her to the Chautauqua circuit.[34]

Among others on the circuit were William Jennings Bryan, the noted political leader and candidate for president, and Dr. Clyde Fisher. The doctor was director of the Hayden Planetarium in New York.[35] Bryan fascinated Te Ata, but Dr. Fisher, although somewhat older, charmed her. And she charmed him. The result was marriage. The couple traveled widely to entertain and be entertained: to Washington, D.C., Chicago, San Francisco, London, Stockholm, and Copenhagen. Their performances continued year after year.[36]

Te Ata returned to rural Oklahoma as often as possible. Relatives and friends remembered her visits to the governor's mansion. "She would sit on the divan," one said, "remove her shoes and relax with her feet propped up. We would talk about 'old times' and about her experiences as an entertainer."

Two of Te Ata's popular programs were "Along the Moccasin Trail" and "The Long Time Ago of the Indians."[37] After Dr. Fisher died, the "Trail" and "The Long Time Ago" drew her back to them. She returned permanently to the Oklahoma City area to be near her sister and niece.[38]

Te Ata's awards included inductions into the Alumni Hall of Fame, University of Science and Arts of Oklahoma, and the Oklahoma Hall of Fame. Also the Chickasaw Hall of Fame. The Roosevelts named a lake in New York "Te Ata," and in 1976 she received the first "Oklahoma Treasure Award." It pertains to "people resources." Governor Henry Bellmon made the presentation.[39] To receive this latter award, one must be seventy years of age, a native or have cultural assents, for which he/she has received prior recognition.[40] More recently, one of Te Ata's legends, "Baby Rattlesnake," was made into a book by another Native American, Lynn Moroney.[41]

Revered by all races and nationalities, Te Ata is nearing the century mark.

MAE BOREN AXTON
(1914-   )
"Queen Mother of Country Music"

The name "Boren" strikes a chord in more ways than one, and they all harmonize. Besides music, it reverberates education, politics, religion, and the humanities. The name "Axton" sounds of sports, especially football, and entertainment. Mae Boren Axton echoes them all.[42] Having composed more than two hundred songs, she became an ambassador of country music many years ago and now spends full time in that profession. After a background in classical music and writing a pop song first, Mae switched to country in 1951. She was the first woman rock and roll writer in America.[43]

Mae is an ex-teacher, a political and religious enthusiast, an aid to friends in need and an author of at least four books.[44] Currently she operates a public relations business in Hendersonville, Tennessee. That includes the guiding force behind a lot of country music stars.

Switching back—World War II found Mae a wife, mother of two small, rollicking boys, and a teacher in Western Oklahoma. "Uncle Sam" found her husband John working in the post office at Fort Sill, Oklahoma. He was taking time out from coaching in that area's schools. John's training for military service began. Mae's training as a military wife began. He moved from base to base on short notice, leaving Mae to pay bills, pack, dispose of the property, or cancel rent.[45] When she had cut all the ties, Mae would take the boys and a load of necessities in the small car and wheel after him.

Mae Boren Axton about 1991. Now living in Hendersonville, Tennessee, she was raised and educated in Oklahoma. She continues to write songs and operate a public relations office. (Courtesy Mae Boren Axton)

Celebrating in 1956 with Elvis Presley is Mae Boren Axton, who helped compose "Heartbreak Hotel," Presley's first record to reap large sales. (Courtesy Mae Boren Axton)

Sometimes the trek led from coast to coast.

When John boarded a ship to the South Pacific, Mae returned to the classroom. She was usually in the speech and English department in high school, but she could fill any vacancy. One of her co-workers at Butner Union Graded in the Seminole County oil fields once remarked, "Mae could sit at her desk writing poetry, and her students would learn more than mine would with me working like a master over them."[46]

"She could leave the room," the co-worker continued, "and her students never made a sound. Mine squawked like jaybirds with me working beside them. I had first grade, while Mae had second. The entire student body loved her. The seniors even chose her as their sponsor, and she directed the senior play.

"We worked together in primary music. We had a toy band, wrote and directed such programs as a circus and 'Cinderella,' all with music."[47]

As far back as that, Mae got the tag, "Queen of the Rockers." Jacksonville, Florida, seems to have been her lucky base. While teaching and writing successful pop-rock songs there, she and a friend co-wrote the classic song "Heartbreak Hotel" for a young, Mississippi-born singer from Memphis, Tennessee, whom a disc jockey, Bob Neal, wanted to manage. His name was Elvis Presley.[48] The song, a 1956 million-selling record, remains one of the all-time biggest sellers year after year.

Elvis, just out of high school, was driving a truck for thirty-five dollars a week to help his parents, who devoted their lives to their only child. His mother Gladys worked as a domestic. His dad did odd jobs—any work he could get.[49] When he could, Elvis would sing for a few dollars or for free. Then Bob Neal heard his first number for Sun Records, one that Elvis had paid to record in the studio as a present for his mother's birthday. It cost him three dollars.

That was when Neal called Mae and other friends around the country for help to get Presley on shows for twenty-five dollars a night. Or whatever could be worked out.[50] "I told Neal," Mae said, "to send him next week. I could get him three dates for fifty dollars a night. I did it for Neal, because I didn't even know Presley at that time.

"When he drove up in his old clunker," Mae continued, "I felt sorry for him. I bought dinner for him, Scotty Moore, and Bill Black and paid for their first night's hotel room in Jacksonville. They paid for their own the next nights in Orlando and Daytona Beach."[51] Mae encouraged Presley, as she encouraged all young people. So did a vice president of RCA Records. He bought Presley's contract from Sun and took the composition, "Heartbreak Hotel." "It catapulted him to fame," Mae said, "reaching a million." The rest of Presley's story belongs to the gods.

When Mae met Presley, she was doing some publicity for several stars, including the noted Hank Snow and some of the characters on "Grand Ole Opry." Burning candles on both ends and in the middle, Mae continued teaching intermittently, writing songs, and helping launch the careers of unknown musicians. They included Willie Nelson, Mel Tillis, and Waylon Jennings. Also, Reba McEntire, Wanda Jackson, Patsy Cline, Roger Miller, Dolly Parton, Kenny Rogers, Crystal Gayle, Lee Greenwood, Jim Reeves, Sonny James, Jerry

Below: Like Mother, Hoyt Axton writes songs, sings, acts, and does art work. His numerous compositions include "Joy to the World" and "Greenback Dollar." His movies include Gremlins. *(Photo courtesy Mae Boren Axton)*

Reed, and many others. The others included Mae's son Hoyt Axton.[52]

When he was a child, he learned to love singing from his father, but it was after Hoyt became a student and football player at Oklahoma State University that he considered music as a career. He became interested in folk, rock, and country types.[53] He began in 1958 in the San Francisco Bay area, then went through the usual struggles of maturation and reaching for success. That came in 1964 when the rock group Steppenwolf heard him sing "The Pusher" and recorded it. The song reached four gold albums and resulted in another recording.[54]

One success led to another. Numerous artists sang Hoyt's compositions "Joy to the World" (not the Christmas carol), "The Pusher," "Never Been to Spain," "Della and the Dealer," "Greenback Dollar," and the "No No Song."[55] Hoyt became an accomplished actor, both on television and in the motion picture theater. These have included The Black Stallion, Liar's Moon, The Junkman, Endangered Species, and Heart Like a Wheel. Also Gremlins, Skinflint, and Country Christmas Carol. The list goes on and on into the talk shows.[56] The latter include Dinah Shore, Mike Douglas, and The Tonight Show. Added to all that are his advertising, art work, and participation in benefits. He has made appearances throughout the United States and several foreign countries. Hoyt Axton's abilities increased with the years.

While that was happening, the other rollicking "little" Axton, Johnny, became a lawyer. His office is in Ada, Oklahoma. Noted far and wide as an excellent attorney, he is credited with forthrightness, cordiality, and—best of all—honesty.[57]

After the boys grew to manhood, Mae returned to East Central University, her alma mater, for a master's degree in psychology and education. At that time, husband John had been out of the Navy a long time and retired from coaching at Broken Bow, Oklahoma.[58]

While driving back to Broken Bow for a weekend on December 2, 1972, Mae was injured in a wreck. That slowed her career, but did not stop it.[59] She recuperated, graduated, and moved to the main site of action in Tennessee. This charged her with more vigor and success. Then husband John's death struck a discord, as all deaths do, but life had to continue. So did Mae's honors and awards. These include a Distinguished Alumni Award from East Central University, speaker at the University's commencement exercise, recognition as Outstanding Oklahoman, and induction into the Oklahoma Women's Hall of Fame. The state legislature declared a "Mae Boren Axton Day" with award.[60]

She has amassed nine BMI Awards for song writing, received the Tex Ritter Award from International Fan Clubs, was named Outstanding Tennessean, was included several times in *Who's Who of American Women*, received a Special Award from Nashville Songwriters' Association International, The Golden Tree Award, an award as Songwriter of the Decade and the Kentucky Colonel Award.[61]

In 1988 the U.S. House of Representatives in Washington, D.C., paid tribute to Mae for her long involvement in the Spina Bifida Association and her contributions to it. That association deals with birth defects of the spine. In Nashville, Mae was affectionately branded "Queen Mother of Country Music."[62]

Mae was born in Texas in 1914. The only girl with eight ambitious brothers, she had to vie for a place in the "chorus." Her parents were "salt of the earth." Very religious, honest, and hard workers, they held high ideals for themselves and their children. They moved to Lawton, Oklahoma, where Mae entered first grade at Lincoln Elementary School. Sometime later the Borens moved to Roff, a small, farm community between Ada and Sulphur. She graduated from high school, then entered East Central University.

Mae's friends remembered her as a brilliant, fun-loving extrovert, sometimes impish, but bound to succeed. She became a champion debater and the object of a handsome athlete's affection. He was John Axton from Broken Bow. Their meeting climaxed in marriage. The two graduated and hit the trail to seek work.[63] The Great Depression was raging. Many graduates could not find jobs, but Mae and John did—she as a teacher and he as a coach. Salaries ranged from seventy-five to one hundred dollars a month for eight-or-nine-month terms. Coaches drew a bit more.[64]

Hoyt and Johnny were born, then World War II took control. It created a generation of transients. Their battles against poverty switched to battles with weapons, either producing or killing with them. That was the nation's lament when the Axtons went to war.

Mae's "rondo" would be incomplete without a note about those eight ambitious brothers and their descendants, all of whom are very close in harmony. They became teachers, ministers, artists, a college president, lecturers, writers, a postal employee, a governor-United States senator. And there are drums beating for one to become president of the United States.[65] No doubt that "salt of the earth" couple out there among the stars are smiling down upon their progeny and singing the "Hallelujah Chorus."

****

Entertainers depend on writers—creators, that is, either themselves or others—for their material. The late Professor Foster Harris of Oklahoma University once said, "There are only three plots for short stories, and they are in the Bible." That book is rich in other types of literature: poetry, proverbs, history. Surprisingly, one authority theorized that Priscilla might have co-authored the book of Hebrews with her husband, Aquila. Women writers in young America were few, but have increased in number tremendously, especially in Oklahoma. Its first playwright was a woman. Space dictates recognition of only three writers in the next chapter.

Chapter 10
WRITERS

LOUISE DALE NELSON
(about 1907-   )
Reviver of Lost Art

It has been said that a book is a "brainchild." In the case of George and Louise Dale Nelson of Mountain Park, Oklahoma, it was also a "child of brawn." Their books of poetry were completely handcrafted in the little workshop at their country home.[1] Their second production, *Fall Crop*, ninety-five pages, came off the press in 1975. Their first, *When the Heart Speaks*, appeared in 1968 and has gone into its sixth printing.

The story of this dual operation is one to warm the heart and fill the soul with admiration for a retired, farmer-teacher-Civil Service couple who made their golden years a period of creativity and production. And they were genuinely happy doing so.[2]

Louise wrote the poems, many of which had been published or had won prizes in Oklahoma and Texas poetry contests. The subject matter was taken from life around the old homestead: the family, the flora, the fauna, and the history of their area.[3] Wherever Louise was—resting beneath the old elm tree or doing chores—she got inspirations

Below: Could they have been the parents of desktop publishing? They are George and Louise Dale Nelson in their tiny Trumpet Vine Press at Mountain Park in 1967. Louise wrote the poetry and helped George on the small press. (Courtesy the Nelsons)

for poems. When she did, she went to her sunlit study in the back of the house and began to write.[4] The length of her poems ranged from three-line Haiku to four-page narratives. The chronology dated from the devastating tornado at nearby Snyder in 1905, which was told to her, to the present.

A thread of reverence for God, life, and integrity laced them all together, and the reader was never left wondering, "What's it all about?" The imagery was clear, crisp and picturesque. Consider the poem "Fall Crop." Taken from the book, *When the Heart Speaks*, its message pertained to the couple's last child Naomi. It proved so popular, the couple chose it as the title and lead poem for their second book.[5]

> We were plowing out the turnrows,
> Our crop about laid by,
> We previewed approaching autumn
> With a melancholy sigh.
>
> The years had passed so very fast,
> Our fledglings, now full grown,
> Were trying out their wings for size,
> And soon we'd be alone.
>
> But Indian summer brought a gift,
> Born on a gentle breeze,
> And dropped a rosebud in our laps,
> The Day before the Freeze.
>
> Again the years have swiftly passed,
> Sweet perfume fills the room,
> The doorbell rings and there she goes,
> Our "Fall Crop" is in bloom.

Another gem with a different glitter is "Cow Council" from the Nelsons' second book. In disgust at the national news of 1974, Louise left the television and went to the kitchen to wash the dishes. Looking out the window, she saw several cows grazing at the foot of the Wichita Mountains. How contented they were and what a contrast between them and the newsmakers. The scene became a seed; the seed began to germinate.[6] In a little while it was in full bloom. She went to her study and began to write:

COW COUNCIL

How serene and free from taxing—
imperturbably relaxing,
it is to watch a herd of cows
graze undisturbed by all the "News."

The red, the yellow, black or white
all bed together every night,
unperturbed that blood is mixed
or that no hybrid strain is fixed.

No worry whether fenced or lib'ed
or genes by which her calf is rib'ed.
She licks him once and chews her cud
and wouldn't change him if she could.

Dappled brown or motley brindle
Jew or Gentile does not kindle
discussion with her little Moo,
on loco weed or poison dew.

Republican or Democrat
left or right-winged plutocrat,
never argue rank or status,
pills that do or don't beget us.

Baptist or Episcopalian
Methodist or sinful hellion
never talk of abrogation
Watergate or Face the Nation —

Except where water-rats for hire
gnawed the lock and tapped the wire,
where breachy cows got out to graze
forbidden oats and other hays.

Daylight Saving Time or Sunday,
holidays now changed to Monday,
concern but little bovine grazing
in my pasture, it's amazing —

How serene and free from taxing,
imperturbably relaxing
it is to watch a herd of cows
graze undisturbed by all the "Nows."

When there were enough poems for an average-sized book, the Nelsons ordered the best paper and book cloth they could get and started production.[7] Their seat of operation was a former milk house, christened The Trumpet Vine Press. That was for the trumpet vines springing up and tumbling over the frame building, almost hiding it from the outside world. But lights were plentiful inside. They set the type with tweezers and printed the pages on

Shown here is Louise Dale Nelson hard at work in her library at Mountain Park in 1967. (Taken by the author)

a small letter press. The signatures were hand-sewn with dental floss on nylon cords of exceptional strength. George did the molding, gluing, and pressing on boards; looms and presses he improvised.[8] The simplicity of the tools reminded the observer of tinker toys, but they were ingenious, and the results were as professional as those of the modern commercial houses.

Not only did the Nelsons write and print their books, but also they did their own public relations and distribution, depending on word of mouth to increase the sales. And it did. They presented programs far and near. Louise lectured, often telling the story of their operation, and recited her poetry. The audiences loved it. George presided at the book table and assisted his wife when they gave a demonstration. Besides appearances throughout Oklahoma, the Nelsons presented programs in Texas, Nevada, New Mexico, Mississippi, and Illinois. The one at the University of Illinois, Urbana, was national in scope. The one at Starkville, Mississippi, was a gathering of some one thousand members of the Mississippi Extension Homemakers' Council. All book sales zoomed after each program.[9]

Natives of Southwest Oklahoma and products of Oklahoma schools, George and Louise met while teaching at Friendship, near Altus in Jackson County. He was principal, and she taught fifth and sixth grades. In 1926 they married in the Dale home, a story within itself. The couple maintained their home in the community where they taught until the death of Louise's father in 1931. They then came back to Mountain Park to help Mrs. Dale with the farm, and there they stayed.[10] George became assistant postmaster and then rural mail carrier, a job he held until 1967. During those years they reared three children: Patsy Ruth, now Mrs. Brice Stogsdill, of Grand Prairie, Texas; Vaughn Dale of Elko, Nevada; and Naomi, "Fall Crop," who is Mrs. Raymond Brown of Athens, Texas.[11]

With their children grown and married, they began dreaming of a new life which would produce different fruit. Having come from a pioneer family of literary bent, one of whom was the late Dr. E.E. Dale, noted historian at the University of Oklahoma, Louise wanted to write.[12] She had been having a "clandestine" affair with poetry, but just before Christmas of 1962 she confessed to George. She read a greeting to family and friends.

"Mom," George said, "that's plum good."

"Do you think," Louise asked, "we could afford to have it printed for our Christmas cards?"

"We'll have it printed," he answered, and they did.

After that, Louise included some of her poems in lectures. The audiences asked for copies, and from their request sprang the idea of the books.[13] "I began an intensive study of form and technique" Louise said. "I attended a writers' class at Tipton, conducted by Vera Holding." Vera and her husband published the Tipton paper, and she wrote books. "At Dr. Dale's advice, I attended the Annual Writers' Conference at the University."[14] That was followed by other schools of instruction, including the Mildred I. Reid Workshop in New Hampshire. Louise joined Pen Women as a lecturer, the Oklahoma Writers' Federation, and the Great Plains Writers' Club at Lawton. She got and gave help wherever she went.

Besides studying, Louise subscribed to writers' magazines. In *Writers' Digest*, she noticed an ad, "How to Print a Book in Your Own Bedroom." It was written by Sidney Elizabeth Blount of Altus, Oklahoma, only a few miles away. The Nelsons ordered the book. After reading it, George declared that was what he wanted to do when he retired. He did not like to fish or play golf. He wanted to do something worthwhile, something creative.

The little booklet of Sidney's prompted the couple to read everything they could find on printing and binding. By George's seventieth birthday, he was ready to retire and renew the almost lost art of hand printing.[15] Louise had enough poetry and comments for ninety-nine pages, so on August 1,

1967, they began work. By January 18, 1968, they had turned out 310 copies of *When the Heart Speaks*. In February the book was offered to the public, and in six weeks it was sold out.[16] The second and third printings brought the total number of copies to 1,683. They were sold out by October 15, 1971. The Nelsons began their fourth printing on September 27, and by November 28, 510 more copies were finished. The selling price was five dollars each. Their fifth and sixth printings followed.

Fall Crop, a product of 1975, is mindful of a bride's Bible. The little white book of cleanliness, half-arched with a trumpet vine in gold, is worthy to be carried down the aisle of any sanctuary.[17]

Louise lost her dear companion/co-worker a few years later and went west to be near her "Fall Crop."

JENNIE HARRIS OLIVER
(1880s-   )
Enchanted Author—Inspiration to All

Poet-author, Jennie Harris Oliver was a celebrity long before most current writers (1992) in Oklahoma were born. And she helped many of the present older writers of the state to success.[18]

One of the most unusual facts about Jennie was her lack of formal education. She and her three brothers "never got beyond the sixth or seventh grade in school. Our father," Jennie said, "was a Baptist minister, who never stayed in one place long enough for us to get school books."[19] However, the family had a large library, and Jennie "read everything in it." She absorbed all that, plus religion, integrity, and a love for life. In addition, she studied nature's way during walks hand-in-hand with her mother. She interwove her experiences with her great imagination to produce books of poetry and fiction.

A native of Lowell, Michigan, Jennie and her siblings "attended schools there." Their father died in that state. In 1898, Mrs. Harris brought the children to Indian Territory and took a homestead in Shiloh.[20] That small community lay about sixteen miles southeast of Guthrie. Jennie secured a position as teacher. By that time, Oklahoma Territory was well enough organized to require teachers' certification. It is, therefore, presumed that Jennie passed an examination. Three years later, she married one of her students, Lloyd Oliver. They established a home in another small community, Fallis.[21] Located among blackjack-studded hills, some fif-

A beloved poet during the first half of this century, Jennie Harris Oliver clowns with a young friend. He is "proposing" to her in her garden at Fallis. Jennie was hosting the annual awards for Oklahoma State Writers. (From the author's collection)

teen miles northeast of Edmond, Fallis is now somewhat of a ghost town, but it is growing. In 1980 it had a population of twenty-two. In 1990, there were forty-nine inhabitants, an increase of more than 122 percent.[22]

Jennie had always wanted to write—to express her love of life and her enchantment with beauty. In Fallis, she came in contact with a younger woman who had the same fantasies. She was Vingie Eve Roe.[23] The daughter of a local physician, Vingie had left school at grade six because of poor eyesight. She spent much of her time riding her horse over the prairies and racing with her dog. She gave vent to inward stirrings by writing and encouraged Jennie to do the same.

Both gained early success as poets, short story writers, and eventually book authors. Vingie moved to California where she lived when her first novel hit the markets in 1912. Its title was *Maid of the*

Whispering Hills. She produced several more after that.[24]

Jennie remained in Fallis. Using her two fingers, she pecked stories on a borrowed typewriter —an old and rickety machine. When she sold one to Muncy Publications, she was enthralled. Muncy published several magazines, including the popular old *Argosy*. That company bought several more of Jennie's stories; then, like all other writers, she hit a dry spell. She wrote, mailed and paced to the post office.[25] "When I got a rejection slip," she said one time, "I was so disappointed and ashamed, I went home the back way to avoid talking with anyone."

Jennie shut herself back into her world of enchantment and worked harder.[26] Then came sales to *Delineator*, *Gunter*, *Holland's*, and *Woman's World*. *Good Housekeeping* became interested in her story based on the "Easter Pageant" in the Wichita Mountains. The editor sent a representative to the area to authenticate that there was such a performance in Oklahoma. When satisfied there was, he bought Jennie's story.[27] In the 1930s Metro-Goldwin-Mayer bought Jennie's Mokey stories for Jackie Cooper. Her books of poetry and fiction included *It is Morning*, *Mokey*, *Oklahoma Poems*, *Pen Alchemy*, *Red Earth*, and *The Singing Hand of Joe Fitzpatrick*.[28]

Jennie lost her mother and husband, but did not allow her loneliness to stunt her ambition, love for others, and natural talent. In May 1939 she hosted at her home a picnic for Oklahoma State Writers, of which she was a member.[29] Her frame house with "forty windows" was filled with frontier mementos and scrapbooks of her presentations, state and national awards, and honors. Her magical garden

Below: The home of Jennie Harris Oliver. The sign says, "Here rest thy caravan." It welcomed area writers and guests. (From the author's collection)

swayed with shade trees and red roses on white trelliswork, reflected in a wishing pool.

After the covered dish luncheon on long picnic tables, Joe Fitzpatrick and Jennie sang her composition, "Oklahoma, Sweet Land of My Dreams." Oscar J. Lehrer of Norman wrote the music and published the composition. It sold for fifteen cents a copy.[30] Joe Fitzpatrick, a noted singer, was a character in Jennie's story of the Easter Pageant. The song's first stanza and chorus are:

> I have a land, where redbuds are burning,
> Spring on the hill and a song in the tree!
> I know a place, where the meadows are turning
> Out of bare winter to green ecstasy.
>
> Dear Oklahoma, how ardent thy sunshine; Radiant thy valleys and pleasant thy streams! Can I forsake thee— Ever forget thee?
> No, Oklahoma, sweet land of my dreams.

There are two more stanzas.[31]

Another number on the program the day of the picnic was poetry readings by club member Louis L'Amour. He read some of his original poems. One memorable selection featured an unusual character he had met on a trip around the world.[32] Although the group enjoyed his presentations, little did anyone dream that Louis would reach the heights of success he attained as a Western writer. At that time, he lived in little Choctaw near Oklahoma City and belonged to the Barnes Literary Club.[33]

President of Oklahoma Writers in 1939 was Sallie Hall Lafon. Additional members included Vivian McCullough, Zoe Tilghman, Lillian Delly, Dora Aydelotte, Helene Damberg, Adelia Clifton, Gladys Cooper, Effa Alexander, Opal Hartsell Brown, Bess Mae Sheets, Etoile A. Weir, Rudolph Hill, Mrs. Otto Lucy, Demma Ray Oldham, and many more from all over the state. And most of them plus college students attended the picnic. Jennie's house and garden were overflowing with guests.[34]

The exact date of Jennie's birth and death are not available, but her life extended from the 1880s to about the 1950s. No doubt she met her finality with a song and a zest for eternity.

ADRIENNE COCHRAN HUEY
(1921-)
Woman of Mettle and Diplomacy

Wife of a diplomat, a world traveler, a linguist, a mother, an artist, a writer, and an adventurer,

Adrienne Cochran Huey's heritage and training emerged to guide her in whatever situation arose in whatever country she lived—England, Argentina, India, Panama, then back to the United States and widowhood. She was a paradox of grace and steel.[35]

When her husband, George Owen Huey, entered foreign service as a consul in 1957, the couple lived in College Park, Maryland. They had four daughters—Nancy, Barbara, Shirley, and Peggy— ranging from age four to thirteen years.[36] On their first assignment overseas, the couple took their quartet to England for two years. It did not take Adrienne long to learn that a man's diplomatic service included his wife and even his children in most instances. She began public duties and learned as she served.

The Hueys' next station was Argentina. That one lasted five years, 1960 to 1965. They returned later for a second term of four years. That was in Buenos Aires without the children.[37] Writing in *The Foreign Service Journal*, Adrienne said, "When we were posted to the U.S. Embassy in Buenos Aires in 1974, the panic over terrorists' activities was at its height. Political assassinations were common and every day the newspapers were full of stories about

Below: Adrienne Cochran Huey, wife of diplomat George Huey, had wondering days and fearful nights to fill her memories. (Courtesy Adrienne Cochran Huey)

foreign businessmen being kidnapped off the streets of the city...."[38]

An American oil man had just been released for an estimated ransom of $16 million plus. George Huey, as consul general, was "considered another prime target...." Americans were leaving, and its school was about to go broke for want of students. The Hueys lived in an eighteen-story apartment building. It and the Embassy were surrounded by guards, and "George went to work daily in an armed vehicle. Still there was no real security. Telephones were bugged."[39] That brought on two-way radios and codes. The Hueys' code was "Oklahoma," and their name was "Rodeo."

It was chilling one day when Adrienne picked up the telephone to hear George's assistant scream frantically: "They got Egan!" Adrienne knew that John Egan was a consular agent in Cordoba, some 450 miles northwest of Buenos Aires. His wife, a Bolivian, had reported to the Embassy that a gang of young terrorists had forced their way into the Egan home and dragged John out to a panel truck. The Egans had been without their native guards two days despite their many calls to the police.[40]

George left immediately in the armed car for the Embassy. Adrienne waited in tremors until she heard from him. He and two more staffers had gone to Cordoba. Terrorists had already killed Egan. His funeral would be under guard. No, the women could not come. It would be too dangerous. Poor Mrs. Egan. She would have no support from the Embassy wives. That same day, three policemen in Buenos Aires were killed, and the president of the Supreme Court was kidnapped. The day was branded "Bloody Friday." The murders brought the number of political deaths for 1976 to fifty-six. And it was only February.[41]

The Hueys completed their first assignment in Buenos Aires and began another in New Delhi, India, without their oldest daughter Nancy. She had finished high school and returned to Iowa for college.[42] As was expected of diplomatic wives, Adrienne participated in several native projects. She helped in the school for retarded children. She distributed milk for UNICEF, taught batik (an art for designing cloth) in the YWCA and held classes in her home.

Writing in *The Foreign Service Journal*, Adrienne told of her two most memorable experiences in that strange country. One was locating and ministering to a sick American. He was in a hospi-

Snapped during one of her services as the wife of a diplomat, Adrienne Cochran Huey, second from left, is teaching the art of batik to a class in Panama. (Courtesy Adrienne Cochran Huey)

tal in New Delhi.[43] It took strategy and blessings from God for Adrienne to weave her way through the dismal maze of narrow streets, crowded with cows, carts, and people on bicycles and on foot. A few others driving cars honked fitfully to clear enough space to crowd through.

The hospital was no easier to negotiate. She stumbled in semidarkness from one hutch-like opening to another. Pitiful dregs of humanity reached out to her and begged for help. Adrienne had to pull away and keep going.[44] The thirty-year-old American she sought lay in squalor and deformity on a string bed. Ropes on which to exercise hung from the low ceiling. Malnourished and bearded, the young man had lived in a shallow cave so long he could not stand erect.

Adrienne introduced herself and gave him a bag of toiletries, treats, and magazines. He accepted the gifts with gratitude and a big snaggle-toothed smile. Presently he reached beneath the ragged blue sheet and drew out a wrinkled length of cloth. "I want you to have this," he said and handed it to her. "This scarf and my American passport are the dearest things I have."[45]

Upon close examination, Adrienne discovered that the object was a blue silk scarf, embroidered with silver thread and finished with fringe. She tried to persuade him to keep it. The young man's eyes pleaded as he insisted she take it. Adrienne put the scarf in her now empty bag, thanked him, and said "Goodbye." After it was laundered, it became a beautiful and unforgettable memento for her.[46]

Adrienne's second story concerned an alarming

incident. During dinner on the evening of March 6, 1966, George received an urgent call from the Embassy. He had to leave. Immediately! She walked with him outside, where he mouthed, "Defector!" then climbed into the family station wagon and disappeared into the creepy India night. Trying to be casual before the three girls, Adrienne wondered and worried until the next day. Who could it be? What had happened? Where was George?[47]

When her husband returned, he was in a state of euphoria, sharpened by anxiety. In strictest secrecy he told her, "It was Stalin's daughter, Svetlana Alliluyeva, defecting to the United States." Stunned, Adrienne listened as George explained what had happened. He and others of the Embassy had forged Svetlana's tourist visa, then put her and an escort on a plane for Rome. Adrienne feared the consequences of the intrigue. It could explode into an international crisis and consume the entire family and endanger the Embassy. Neither she nor George breathed easily until they knew the defector had arrived safely in Rome.

Svetlana had been in India for the funeral of her Indian husband and did not want to return to the Soviet Union. She was forced to come to the Russian Embassy in New Delhi and await transport to Russia. Staffers there were having a big party. There was plenty to drink. As some of the Indian women left, Svetlana joined them. Her one suitcase held a manuscript of utmost importance to the West. She made it to the United States, and her book became one of the most sensational of all ages.[48] Adrienne served as a brace for her husband in many trying circumstances. But there were compensations. One was an autographed copy of Svetlana's book, for which they were pleased.

Born in Booneville, Mississippi, in 1921, Adrienne descended from Southern gentlepeople, but they never shrank from reality and adventure. Even from intrigue.[49] Adrienne's great-great grandmother was a horse-galloping spy for the South during the Civil War. Union forces captured her, but she triumphed to survival.[50] Adrienne's parents moved to Dallas when she was small. Their next move was to Oklahoma City. She graduated from Classen High School and attended Oklahoma College for Women (now Oklahoma University of Science and Arts) at Chickasha. World War II fell upon the country, and the "hurry-up-generation" jumped into action.[51]

Adrienne transferred to business college. Her training there qualified her for a position in the Selective Service System, Washington, D.C. In the capital she met George O. Huey, a passport official at the Department of State, where he was to have a thirty-five-year career. The last twenty were in the Diplomatic Service as a consul.[52]

During those two decades overseas, their four daughters sometimes expressed the feeling of being without citizenship. They traveled in many countries outside the ones in which they served. They became world cultured as well as college graduates. The oldest one, Nancy, has a family and lives in Wisconsin. The second, Barbara, is with the Air and Space Museum in Washington, D.C., and has two sons. The third, Shirley, lives and works with her husband in Michigan. The youngest, Peggy, lives in San Diego, California, and is a broker's assistant at Dean Witter.[53]

Adrienne was left alone when her husband died in 1979, but continued to work as a writer, an artist, and a translator for medical missionaries in Ecuador. She has served as an officer in several organizations. A recent interest of hers is the Anthropological Society of Oklahoma. She has gone on digs and found them most fascinating. At present, Adrienne is with her daughter, Nancy, and family in Wisconsin.[54]

****

Literature production became so successful in Oklahoma, it gave birth to publishing. By women. Of course, women had been involved in business since territory days. They kept boarders, operated rooming houses and millinery shops, and managed farms and ranches. They continue to do all that and more. The following four business women are exceptional.

Chapter 11
BUSINESS MANAGERS

EDNA MILLER HENNESSEE
(about 1910-   )
Entrepreneur with Unlimited Dreams

A tour of Edna Miller Hennessee's Cosmetic Specialty Labs, Inc., in Lawton, Oklahoma, is like a trip through a dairy plant where milk, ice cream, yogurt, and the like are processed for consumption. Or maybe a visit to an enormous bakery.[1] To an ordinary layman, the 180,000-square-foot building is a tangle of cords, pipes, and appliances, hanging from the high ceiling to imprison enormous stainless steel vats and gnarled apparatus in various shapes and sizes. It is mind boggling but gleaming with sterility and wonder. A person could eat from any vessel with safety.[2]

Edna accompanies guests to explain, "Now this is where we make bottles. We take pellets of plastic, make the molds, then...." Her words fade into the tangle of machinery as she leads into another room. "And this is where we make boxes," she says. "We...."[3] Again the explanation fades. The tour leads from one department to another—the mixing vats, the testing tubes, and finally to a storage room. Cardboard boxes are stacked to the ceiling. "All of these," Edna says with a sweep of her hand, "are bound for Malaysia."[4]

That registers! It is understandable, but not understandable. How did she get such a gargantuan order from faraway Malaysia? How did she get any order from Malaysia? That country is halfway around the world—a narrow peninsula diving from Thailand toward the equator like a long-necked goose trying to take a bite out of Singapore.[5]

The wonderment minimizes the rest of the tour. Finally, however, a series of questions and a stack of printed information, plus memories of past association with Edna solve the mystery. It is like a fairy tale, but not without witches.

Edna Hennessee grew up as Edna Miller in Ryan, Oklahoma, graduating as valedictorian of her senior class. Troubled by a teen-age skin problem, she tried a variety of remedies before someone gave her a packet of Merle Norman cosmetics. The product cleared her skin and gave her a subconscious sense of direction.[6] For the time being, however, the girl from Ryan sought a future in Oklahoma City. She got a job as proofreader for the State Legislature.

Prior to World War II, she married Lloyd Hennessee, and they moved to Lawton. She worked as a nurse and later a clerk. The latter job paid $17.50 a week.[7] The war became full-grown on December 7, 1941, with the Japanese attack on Pearl Harbor, and Edna's husband joined the Seabees. She went to work in a defense industry in California. When Lloyd went overseas, Edna returned to Oklahoma and worked at Tinker Air Force Base in Oklahoma City.

Before the war ended, she returned to Lawton. Her prior success with Merle Norman products followed her like a patch of sunshine. It urged her to contact the cosmetic company in California, asking to be a representative in Lawton.[8] The reply stated that the venture would cost more money than Edna had. How could she ever afford it? The dream to become a cosmetologist grew so strong, she told herself, "I will do it somehow. I will do it."

Edna bought a washing machine and began moonlighting. After a day of clerking, she went home to "wet wash" for the public. That meant she washed at night, and customers picked up the wet

Below: Edna Miller Hennessee greets customers Frank and Steve Jones in the laboratory of her Cosmetic Specialty Labs, Inc., at Lawton about 1990. The company is a multimillion-dollar operation which she began with a washing machine in the 1940s. (Courtesy Edna Miller Hennessee)

clothes next morning to hang on their line.[9] After saving three hundred dollars, Edna bought a twelve-dollar bus ticket to Merle Norman Studios in California. She needed at least a thousand dollars to become a representative. A persistent young woman by then, Edna persuaded the Merle Norman officials to let her become an agent. She took the necessary training, finished it early, and returned home to enter business. That was 1944.

World War II ended the next year, and husband Lloyd came home from the South Pacific. The couple had a son and daughter, Marilyn and Odus Miller. The children did not thwart Edna's business and dreams. She wanted to develop her own cosmetics. Using her kitchen as a laboratory, she studied and experimented with chemicals. She met failures with determination, changing formulas and trying again. Finally, she thought she had a winning line and named it for her children, "Marilyn Miller." That demanded more work and acute business management.[10]

The children reached school age, and that added to her duties. She attended PTA meetings, served as homeroom mother, and helped during such special events as Halloween carnivals. Edna's generosity, like her dreams, was boundless. She gave gifts to teachers and provided cosmetics and hair care to residents of nursing homes. She gave freely to other charities—perhaps too freely. Witches intervened.[11] The dreamer met with divorce. Then bankruptcy!

The spurs on her dreams put failure to flight,

and the lady, who began with a washing machine, founded another business—The Hennessee Beauty Academy.[12] This energizing endeavor led to another and another: Cosmetic Specialty Labs, Inc.; Universal Graphics, Inc.; a real estate and brokerage company; and Dream Valley Farm. The farm is a 160-acre plot of prairie near Cache. It supports forty greenhouses, where millions of aloe vera plants grow for Edna's cosmetics and health drink and for market to others.[13]

Edna was so happy with her work, she took time to write a book, *I Don't Have to; I Get To*, and had it illustrated. The more she expanded, the more people took note. Orders came from all over the United States, from Spain, England, Holland, Brunei.... Helen and Jacob Sagamoney from Malaysia came and signed a twelve-year agreement to distribute Edna's cosmetics there and in other countries of the Far East.[14]

Edna travels far and wide to hold seminars and to serve on committees and commissions for private industry, the state, and the nation. Her son Odus, president of the company, also travels. Daughter Marilyn is chairman of the board and secretary-treasurer. "I treat my children," Edna says, "the same way I treat all the other two hundred employees. And I expect the same from them I do from others."[15]

The Cosmetic Specialty Labs and the Hennessee family have been featured in numerous publications. Besides such state papers as *Oklahoma Economic Development News*, their stories have appeared in the *Kansas City Star*, *Nation's Business*, *Savvy* magazine, *Sun Publications*, and many more. They have been interviewed on numerous talk shows for radio and television.[16]

What accounts for such multimillion-dollar enterprises and success? A close observation of Edna Miller Hennessee seems to indicate that she is completely dedicated to business. She is always kind and courteous, but has no time for foolishness—no time to waste. "When I go somewhere (and that is often)," she says, "I am always looking for an opening...for ways to improve my business. And I usually find them. When I improve it, I am helping my customers and we all benefit."[17]

MOLLY SUE LEVITE GRIFFIS
(1938-   )
Publishing Is Her Business

A woman book publisher in Oklahoma? A real

publisher, whose books are not financed by the state, some philanthropist, or the author? How could one be so confident, so courageous, to establish a publishing house this far from big cities, especially New York City?[18] Molly Sue Levite Griffis of Norman—that's who! Her company is Levite of Apache, so called in honor of her parents and the Oklahoma town where she grew up.[19]

The business sprang from a Christmas gift Molly and her sister, Georgann Levite Vineyard, of Lawton gave their father, George Levite, in 1973. It was a box of five hundred small, paperback books titled *By George*. These were a collection of stories about life in a small town. Levite had been a stringer for the *Daily Oklahoman* and the *Lawton Constitution*.[20]

When the daughters presented the books to their father, he asked, "What in the world are we going to do with five hundred books?"

"Sell them, of course," the daughters answered. And sell them they did. Almost immediately. They did a second printing, which proved so popular, the daughters enlarged and reissued it under the title of

Below: Venturing into book publishing in 1973, Molly Levite Griffis works in the office of her company, Levite of Apache, which is located in Norman. (Courtesy Molly Levite Griffis)

By George! for Lilly. Lilly was their mother.[21] That also was successful. But why wouldn't it be? Most of the characters therein were residents or former residents of that community. Others considered it a fascinating history of a small town, somewhat like their own.

Apache had inherited two cultures: that of the prairie Indians and that of a variety of races from other countries. Many were Europeans. The Indians' sedentary life style had been forced upon them, while the others had chosen to settle among them. This often created a carnival-like atmosphere.[22] There were such merchants and settlers as William Lange, a German tailor; F.A. Hrabe, a harness shop operator from Norway; Mr. and Mrs. Peter Herber, owners of the Opera House and a hotel, who were from Luxembourg; Sam Sing, a laundry operator from China; and missionaries from the East Coast of the United States.

The Indians, mostly Apache, Comanche, and Kiowa, were farmers on their allotments. They had such names as Medicine Cow or Crow, Big Shoulders, Bird's Head, Brings Plenty, Two Hatchet, Old Lady Sixteen....[23] Some spoke of their homes as their "sit downs," the oceans as "big creeks," and illegitimate children as "grass babies." They had no "cuss" words in their language. That was explained as being because they "had no bad Indians" to condemn.[24]

That was a small part of the basis for *By George! for Lilly*. The book included some of the Indians' humor, traditions, and philosophies. They practiced polygamy. One was said to have had twelve wives. Many of their statements were wise, even if amusing. One told Levite, "When we go to church, we carry our big bag of sins with us. We leave our bag outside.... We go in, hear preacher preach, sing, and pray, then go out and pick up same bag of sins to carry around till next Sunday."[25]

The town of Apache at that time had the usual sports, entertainments, and high jinks as other frontier communities. There was a basketball team, a band, trains to meet, and schemes to lay. Levite knew all about them.

The town team was playing the Boston Bloomers, supposed to be an all-girls team. Some turned out to be men. Halloween night the town "pests" took a cow upstairs at school. Next morning the janitor discovered it and called for "HELP!"[26] A tent show came to town. Admission was "free," but the cost to get out was ten cents. Another traveler came to town and bought six bars of Crystal White soap for twenty-five cents. He cut them into tidbits, wrapped them in foil and sold each on the streets as "The World's Greatest Spot Remover." The price was twenty-five cents per tidbit.[27]

Levite of Apache's second book was successful, so Molly and Georgann added another and another by different authors. They called them the "Land Series." "When I took my end-of-the-year inventory recently," Molly said in 1990, "I had fewer than fifty of each title. That meant I had sold nearly 30,000 of those funny, saddle-stitched things. I thought I might have flooded the market, so I made a change."[28]

Molly changed to children's books and tried a "double-take." Keeping it historical, she published one volume in both soft and hard covers. The title was *The Remarkable Ride of the Abernathy Boys*. It is the story of the small Abernathy boys from Western Oklahoma who made the trip on horseback to Washington, D.C. They did it without adults. Again success came her way, so she contracted for two more titles in 1991: *Danger on the Homestead* by Tulsa writer Bessie Holland Heck, and *Komantcia* by Norman writer Harold Keith. His was a reprint.[29]

The Levite sisters have additional qualities and positions. Georgann is a teacher in Lawton Public Schools, while Molly is a popular storyteller for children. She appears in public libraries to perform in costume. That is much more entertaining than just telling stories.[30] She is also an expert saleslady. She was nurtured in salesmanship and public relations in the family business in Apache. "Advertising is my least expense," Molly said. "I'm fortunate to get radio, television, and newspaper interviews."

Her grandfather Peter Levite, a Russian Jew, came to America in the late 1800s. He settled in Apache in 1903 when the area was still Oklahoma Territory: raw, rough, and ready, but opportune.[31] He established the Levite Corner Store, which his son George took over in later years. Like his father, George was an honest, hard-working and serious-minded man who loved his family. A self-taught psychologist, George knew his customers as if they wore their traits between their eyes. Often he chuckled about the things they said and did or did not do.

Molly's mother, Lilly, was a Texan, thirteen years younger than George. She was a social-minded woman, involved in the cultural side of her family and the city of Apache. "She was a cracker-jack," Molly said, "lovable, zany, and, as Father used to say, 'About all she ever did at the store was to dust.' She was the only one for him."[32]

Molly graduated from Apache High School and the University of Oklahoma and has done thirty-four hours of postgraduate study. She was a graduate assistant in English at the University and taught eight years in the public schools of Oklahoma.[33] She had been a tour director for foreign students, a programmer for the Oklahoma Department of Libraries, a church worker, a book reviewer and free-lance writer, a clerk at Peyton-Marcus, and an instructor in Hatha Yoga.

Molly's husband, Louis Griffis, was in the military for thirty-five years and works for Kerr-McGee Oil Company. They have two children, George and Ginger.[34] George graduated from the University of Oklahoma in 1990. His last year was spent at the Technical University in Berlin, Germany, on a fellowship. While there he saw the Berlin Wall come down. Ginger attended Tulsa University and, following in the steps of her ancestors, graduated from the University of Oklahoma in business.

FRANKIE SUE GAGE GILLIAM
(1943-)
Woman of Many Facets

Wife, mother, dreamer, business and professional woman, Frankie Sue Gage Gilliam has been it all. Of Cherokee lineage, her latest venture was to reissue the Indian magazine, *Twin Territories*, which hit the market first in October 1898. The last edition came out in 1902 (it cost a dollar a year or ten cents a copy).[35] Frankie Sue's first issue of the revised publication was in 1990. Since then it has appeared nine times a year as a cross-cultural magazine in newsprint. Its cost is $12.50 annually or $1.50 per copy.[36]

Anyone interested in history, travel, genealogy, or art will thrill just to browse through a copy. It features saints and sinners, aristocrats and proletaries, mystics and messengers. Herein are titles of the "Year of the Indian" issue of fifty-six pages: "Kenneth Anquoe, 'The Star' of Anadarko"; "The Pow-Wow Drum"; "Intertribal Dance Competition"; "Battle of Cabin Creek"; "Night Creature"; "One Day Tour"; and "Fort Gibson."[37] *Twin Territories'* line drawings stir the spirit. Its photographs assure authenticity, and its ads snap with attention.

A descendant of the Western Cherokees, first of the Five Civilized Tribes to settle in Oklahoma, Frankie Sue Gage Gilliam reestablished an early magazine, Twin Territories, *in 1990. It earlier had been published from 1898 to 1902. (Courtesy Frankie Sue Gage Gilliam)*

Frankie Sue's staff of eight includes reporters, researchers, and artists.

For a lady who said she knew little if anything about the publishing business, Frankie Sue's success is phenomenal. Her reasons for beginning the venture were necessity, her collection of historical information, and her love of Oklahoma. Quoting another Muskogee publication, *Current*, for January/February 1991, Frankie Sue said, "When you think of the kind of folk that came here and stayed, we have ended up with the strongest and the best, the hardiest stock. People not only survived the hardships of settling, but also the Depression and Dust Bowl. We kept the survivors."

Frankie Sue is a descendant of earlier survivors and is one herself. A native of Fort Gibson, she is the daughter of Frank and Dorothy Gage Gilliam.[38] "They still live on my grandmother's (father's) Cherokee allotment," she said, "and my dad is a farmer-rancher. My mother is a homemaker.... Both are the best." The unity with which she grew up among eight siblings is shown in their "begging" her to move back to Fort Gibson among them.[39]

After finishing Fort Gibson Public Schools, Frankie Sue attended Draughon's School of Business, Bacone College, and Conners State College. She had extensive training in association management and took several independent courses of study. These included the Institute for Organization Management, sponsored by the United States Chamber of Commerce at Southern Methodist University; Realtors' Institute at Oklahoma State University; and the Dale Carnegie Institute. Frankie Sue has been a business woman since 1963. She operated a grocery store, a laundromat, and rental property and had dealerships for United States Suzuki, Subaru, and Triumph.

She became a realtor associate of James Askew Agency and the Gallery of Homes. From 1974 to 1982, Frankie Sue was Executive Director of the Muskogee Board of Realtors. This handed her the responsibility of maintaining procedure on ethics and arbitration hearings.[40] More and more responsibility came her way. In 1982 Frankie Sue became Director of the Convention and Visitors Bureau of Muskogee's Chamber of Commerce. She was manager of the Civic Center with a $300,000 budget and sixteen employees.

Seven years later Frankie Sue was appointed full-time Tourist Director. She enlisted a volunteer force of one hundred persons as docents, tour guides, and Tourist Information Center attendants.[41] All the time, that vital lady was collecting information—current and historical, much of it from her own family. She was making friends...many friends. But the ladder beneath her climb had a broken rung![42]

Early in 1990, the political atmosphere switched directions. A twenty-four-year-old man assumed directorship of the Chamber of Commerce. He directed a steep cut in Frankie Sue's salary. She had twenty years experience in organizational management. "Besides," she said, "I had three youngsters in college and couldn't accept the cut without a supplement in salary." The finale was: the young man fired her!

"I can't tell you," she said, "how hard I prayed for an idea. I tried to think of a product that did not exist in Oklahoma, and the *Tombstone Epitaph* in

Arizona came to mind. That was the answer to my prayer. I would revive *Twin Territories*." It was similar to the *Tombstone Epitaph*. "With no money in the bank, one month's severance pay and scared," Frankie Sue admitted, "I jumped into it. For fear someone might steal my idea, I kept mum about it until I got it underway."[43]

The original magazine had begun under the guidance of Walter and Myrta Eddleman Sams, newspaper publishers in Muskogee at the end of the 19th century. They had persuaded Myrta's sister Ora, only eighteen years old, to write for and edit it. They were part Cherokee. Ora's publication came at a crucial era for the Indians, especially those of the Five Civilized Tribes. They were losing their nations and schools and facing allotments. Those transitions were news stories. So was their culture.[44]

One of Ora's features stated: "There is nothing improper or bold in a young lady allowing her picture to appear in these columns..., and let me say to you, just anybody can't get their picture in *Twin Territories*. She must be a pure-minded, respectable girl."[45]

Before Ora married a reporter for the *Kansas City Star*, she tried to persuade someone to replace

Below: Frankie Sue Gage Gilliam, editor-publisher of Twin Territories, *sits at her desk in Muskogee. She and daughter Julia live at Tahlonteéskee, early capital of the Cherokees. (Courtesy Frankie Sue Gage Gilliam)*

her as editor of *Twin Territories*. No one could be persuaded to take the challenge. Thus, for eighty-eight years that early magazine, originally edited by an eighteen-year-old Indian miss, remained a hidden inspiration that proved a lifesaver for Frankie Sue.[46]

"Most of my friends," she said, "are artists and writers. So are my sisters—all six of them. I have seen them make something wonderful and beautiful and give it away for nothing. I thought I could not only help myself financially, but I could help others develop markets."

Many of those friends and family members, especially her daughter, Julia Etta Kiddie, helped her. Julia Etta's interest in tourism and business began when she was a child, and it continues to increase.[47] She majored in those fields, plus marketing at Northeastern State University in Tahlequah, from which she graduated in 1993. While a senior on a scholarship, Julia Etta planned, developed and produced the "14 Flags Festival." It was presented at the Muskogee Exposition site.[48] All the while, she was helping her mother with *Twin Territories*.

Julia Etta would like to see a bus tour of historic sites in Northeast Oklahoma. They would include such places as Muskogee, Tahlequah, and Fort Gibson. She believes the tour would make a wonderful attraction.

The daughter-mother heritage lies in at least two notable persons of history: Hercules Terrapin Martin, interpreter for Indian agent Montford Stokes, and Daniel Boone, warrior, trailblazer, and hero. Three others in the family are equally blessed. They include "Lisa and Freddie Kiddie and John Marsden, all of Muskogee."[49]

Frankie Sue admits that publishing is hard work, and sometimes statements in the stories are disputed. Some readers will write: "It didn't happen that way at all...." Then she receives a box full of "new subscriptions from all over the world," mixed with encouraging messages. They eclipse the negatives and hours of hard work.[50] "I'm determined to hold on," she said, "and be on the cutting edge.... I hope to market Oklahoma artists, craftsmen, writers, etc. I dream of a company like 'Leaning Tree' in Colorado."

Frankie Sue has a wonderful place to dream. She and daughter Julie now reside at historic Tahlonteeskee, near Gore, Oklahoma, where Julie is site director. Frankie Sue will volunteer her spare time at the Cherokee courthouse.[51] Their ancestors settled there, when they entered Indian Territory, and helped establish the Cherokee Nation. Hercules Terrapin was clerk in the Senate. The place remained the Cherokee capital until 1843 when it was moved to Tahlequah. Overflowing with beauty, interest, and intrigue, Tahlonteeskee will, no doubt, be the subject of many articles in future issues of *Twin Territories*.[52]

JANE MILLER HARDIN
Business Is Her Business

Almost any time, seven days a week, one can find Jane Miller Hardin on the job at 17 South Dewey in Oklahoma City, flying high above the clouds to some out-of-state gathering, or granting interviews to the print or electronic news media. She is Executive Director and Certified Officer of Central Oklahoma's Better Business Bureau.[53] Jane is the first woman in Oklahoma to hold that position and one of the first in the United States to head a Better Business Bureau.

Her job is to direct all phases of Bureau operations. She works with business, industry, civic and educational groups and the public in general.[54] When someone is accused of operating a scam, using highhanded tactics or engaging in commercial dishonesty in any form, Jane and her staff waste no time reviewing the accusations. She listens to the charges and denials, keeps records, and makes decisions.

As editor of the *BBB Newsletter* and conductor of seminars, Jane alerts consumers and distributors about unethical people and their practices. She monitors advertising and is co-producer of the television series, "Money and You."[55] Jane hosts the regular meetings of the Better Business Bureau and serves on a multiplicity of boards, associations and councils. Among the communication organizations she has served as president are the Oklahoma Branch of the National League of American Pen Women and Oklahoma Press Women, an affiliate of the National Federation of Press Women. The first time Oklahoma Press Women chose her "Woman of Achievement," Jane ranked second in the National Contest. She will represent Oklahoma again in 1993 at Kansas City.[56]

Jane was well-qualified to head the Better Business Bureau in 1977. She started in that direction when she began operating a restaurant in Oklahoma

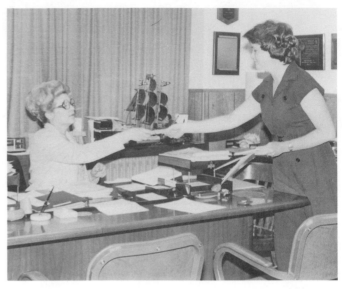

Director of the Better Business Bureau in Oklahoma City, Jane Miller Hardin is shown presenting a Certificate of Completion to a young woman who worked as an apprentice under her supervision. (Courtesy the Better Business Bureau, Oklahoma City)

City. In addition, she taught commercial subjects at Hill's Business University, lectured at St. Luke's School of Continuing Education, and monitored the State Test for the Oklahoma State Personnel Board.[57]

Some thirty-three years ago, Jane became an employee of the Better Business Bureau. Her initial position included Consumer Consultant Manager, Trade Practice Consultant, Assistant Manager-Director; then she assumed the top position. At the time she took over, the organization rented space in a downtown office building. She and the Board of Directors decided to save money by moving to another location. It was less desirable, but not for long.[58] Jane and a few others spent incalculable hours renovating the building and creating an appealing atmosphere.

The organization took on new growth and more responsibility. One was the Arbitration Program. Jane's husband Kenneth L. Hardin became director.[59] When a customer has a complaint against a company, such as an automobile dealer, the complainant and a representative of the company agree to discuss their problem before an arbiter. Hundreds of cases are settled in that manner.[60]

When the Better Business Bureau outgrew the facilities, the membership decided to buy property. After many self-examinations, location considerations, and economic appraisals, they bought a larger building at a bargain. It was in a blighted

Jane Miller Hardin shows one of the numerous awards she has received. Others line the walls of her office. (Courtesy Better Business Bureau, Oklahoma City)

area, but again not for long.[61] Jane rolled up the "sleeves" of her determination, recruited helpers, and worked harder than ever. In a matter of months the crew had renovated and furnished the seven-thousand-square-foot brick building with first-class office equipment. That included a new computer system. Plants, pictures and spongy carpet added sunshine to the decor and seemed to smile a welcome to the Better Business Bureau. Not only that, but blight in the neighborhood began disappearing: restructuring, fresh paint, and new buildings began to appear.[62]

Membership in 1993 reached seventeen hundred, forty-onc of whom were board members, and seventeen were on the staff. There were 102 volunteers. The year before, the organization reached a revenue of more than half a million dollars, and is working for a greater one.[63] The largest project is to complete installation of a super network of electronic equipment. It will operate worldwide. If someone in Chicago wants information about a company in Oklahoma, for example, an employee will have it at his/her fingertips.[64]

How does one succeed as Jane Miller Hardin has succeeded? With the "aim of preventing crime and raising the standards of ethics in business practices," she is completely dedicated to her job. "I can't think of any morning," she said, "when I got up and hated to go to work." She does that with such grace and calmness, she never seems angry or frustrated.[65]

A native of Clayton, Oklahoma, Jane is the daughter of Ted and Ruby Miller. She attended public schools at Clayton and Davidson, Oklahoma, then took advanced education and training at the University of Oklahoma and Oklahoma City University.

She completed a scholarship in the Southwest College of Consumer Finance, graduated in Executive Management Training from Washington University, St. Louis, Missouri, from Oklahoma Securities Fraud Seminar, and several others.[66] Her husband, Kenneth L. Hardin, was in the law brief printing business before he became director of the Arbitration Program. They have a son, Steven L. Hardin. He graduated from Oklahoma State University as a certified public accountant and started his career in Dallas, Texas, but returned to work in Oklahoma.[67] Religiously, Jane is a Presbyterian. She was always devoted to her parents. After the loss of her father, she drew nearer to her mother as a protector and friend.

What advice would Jane give a young woman interested in becoming a director of such an organization as the Better Business Bureau? "I would tell her," she said, "if you want to be better than the best, you have to work harder than the best." Jane Miller Hardin, whose impeccable grooming reflects her philosophy of excellence, not only says that—she lives it.[68]

****

Inasmuch as science is a synonym for reason and knowledge, women have been active in that field for millenniums. The word hygiene comes from the Greek goddess of health, Hygeia.[69] The primitive Indian women helped tame the land and explore the forests for plants with medicinal properties. Women transformed grain into bread and flax into linen.[70] Indian women were doctors, although some observers tagged them "witch women." They had a secret method of preventing pregnancy. When they did bear babies, they went to a private house or beneath a tree in complete isolation from men.[71] They had to be knowledgeable to do all those things and more.

In France, Mme. Marie Sklodowska Curie received the Nobel Prize in chemistry. Women everywhere, certainly here in Oklahoma, have contributed their share of knowledge and expertise to the improvement of humanity, as the reader can see in the next chapter.

Chapter 12
SCIENTISTS-REASONERS

SALLIE LEWIS STEPHENS STURGEON
(1870s-1955)
Woman Paradox

A journalist and the first woman health inspector in the United States, Sallie Lewis Sturgeon was an antisuffragist. She demanded that communities and individuals "clean up or close up," yet she opposed women's privilege of real citizenship. Her constituents opposed her. At first.[1]

A native of Missouri, Sallie and her husband Thomas H. Sturgeon came to Oklahoma City in 1894, then moved to Ardmore a few years later. He worked first for the Santa Fe railroad, then in the Ardmore National Bank. Lee Cruce was president of the bank.[2] Sallie took a job on the local newspaper, *The Statesman*, then transferred to the *Daily Ardmoreite*. It was there she established a full page of news for women, covering everything from etiquette to poetry to noted American women.[3]

The popularity of her work led to the establishment of a magazine, *The Oklahoma Lady*, in 1908. Issued weekly at five cents a copy, this was the first magazine for Oklahoma women.[4] Sallie patronized the women's clubs of the entire state. Their membership numbered into the hundreds of thousands, and their activities were equally numerous. Features in *The Oklahoma Lady* included such topics as entertainment, biographical sketches, and fashions. It stressed the need for men to vote the best qualified men into office..., those who would clean up crime.[5] Sallie sold the publication to Blanche D. Lucas of Guthrie, who eventually discontinued it.[6]

In 1910, Lee Cruce won the nomination to become Oklahoma's second governor. He took Sallie's husband to Oklahoma City as an aide. The two were involved in the oil business, as well as politics.[7] The Sturgeons moved to Oklahoma City where Sallie established a news bureau. This increased her activities and opposition to women's suffrage. Two other outstanding women in the state worked with her: Alice Robertson and Kate Bernard, which seemed as paradoxical as Sallie inasmuch as both held public office.[8]

But they and their followers went down in defeat—actually by a small majority. The 19th Amendment to the Constitution passed in 1920, stating in part, "The right of citizens of the United States to vote shall not be denied or abridged by the United States or any state on account of sex...."[9]

Sallie lost her husband in 1919. A year later, Gov. J.B. A. Robertson appointed her inspector for the Oklahoma State Health Department. Opposition was bitter. A woman could not do a job like that; men would run her off the place![10] Seeming to ignore the insults, Sallie steeled herself and bent to it. She employed trains, jitneys, and her own two feet to transport herself from town to town. She inspected whole sections: hotels, restaurants, alleys, jails, rooming houses, livery stables....

Below: After a career in most everything except women's suffrage, Sallie Lewis Stephens Sturgeon was appointed inspector for the Oklahoma State Health Department in 1920. Despite much opposition, she succeeded. (Courtesy Oklahoma Historical Society)

Some of the things she discovered would revolt the strongest stomach and haunt the owner's sleep. Hogs ran loose in the streets, privies and barns went uncleaned, food spoiled, dirty mattresses harbored bedbugs, worms feasted on candy.[11] One man with sore hands mixed hamburgers; another cleaned vegetables with a knife he had used to cut a bunion from his foot. The number and types of health violations were limitless, but Sallie bore up with patience and determination.

Then the Depression hit, adding deep poverty to ignorance. Unemployed and destitute people took refuge in squatters' camps around the country, usually along streams. They stretched tents, hammered junk into hovels, or existed without either under the skies during sun and storms.[12] Oklahoma City had a camp, often called "Hooverville." It was on the north bank of the North Canadian River. With very little food and water and no sewage facilities, thousands of people gathered in squalor. The City had to act.

Its officials and humanitarian organizations came up with a "make work" program. They sponsored a community of small houses with sewer facilities, a school and clinic. Workers on the city program made from $5.00 to $7.50 a week. Sallie "fell heir" to the job of social worker for settlers in the community. The project became so successful, officials from other states took note and fashioned their own after it. Sadly enough for the progenitors of the program, it succumbed to the New Deal. Complimentary, however, the New Deal is said to have been based on the one it replaced.[13]

Sallie died in 1955, but her monumental contribution to the state of Oklahoma lives on. Furthermore, this lady from the "Show Me" state did just that—she proved to her detractors that she could handle a man's job and handle it boldly.

GERTRUDE SOBER FIELD
(1869-1949)
Geologist, Miner, and More

Labeled "Queen of the Arbuckles" by a Mr. Woodward of the United States Department of Interior, Gertrude Sober Field seemed to have been born with an interest in geology and mining long before women were accepted in such positions. And she did many more types of work to prove her mettle.[14]

While working in Oklahoma City as a secretary to a couple of legislators, Gertrude heard reports from Professor Charles N. Gould of the University of Oklahoma and others about riches in the Arbuckle Mountains. The professor took his students there in a wagon and camped for regular study.[15] These stories sharpened Gertrude's interest. She took a hammer and a geologist's kit, mounted a horse, and went forth alone to prospect. That was about 1907.

Choosing a rocky wilderness in the vicinity of the Butterly Ranch, eight miles west of Davis, Gertrude set up a primitive camping facility and began chipping at formations for minerals. Her presence in the area was soon discovered, and others became interested.[16] An elderly physician in Davis, Dr. R.C. Hope, became a financier and joined in the search for minerals. That led to the organization of the Indian Mining and Development Company. Other officials included: D.B. Welty and A J. McMahan of Oklahoma City and T.H. Slover of

Gertrude Sober Field in 1911 with the tools of her profession. Her pick and work clothes clearly indicate her profession. (Courtesy Mildred Sober West)

99

In sharp contrast to her work clothes, Gertrude Sober Field here is in her Sunday hat (about 1910). (Courtesy Mildred Sober West)

Davis. They sold stock at one dollar a share and reportedly operated on a million-dollar fund.

Gertrude moved into an abandoned log cabin. Traveling on her horse and by foot, she toiled and sacrificed for two years before she discovered zinc-producing earth. When the company decided that there was sufficient ore worth mining, employees hauled it to the Santa Fe railroad in Davis for shipment to smelters.[17]

Early in the mining project, two young brothers, Roy and Chester Field, came looking for work and found it. They had little formal education, so Gertrude shared her learning with them. She became devoted to Chester, twenty-three years her junior, and he became devoted to her. This teacher-student relationship lasted several years, finally culminating in deep love. They were married in January 1918, but tragically not for long.[18] World War I was raging and the United States was drawn into it. Chester went into military service and got as far as Camp Dix, New Jersey, where he succumbed to the epidemic of Spanish Influenza then raging. The War Department returned his body to Davis. He was buried in Oak Ridge, a nearby cemetery.[19] Gertrude never remarried. She increased her work and study for solace.

A native of Iowa, her parents were Captain Morris and Isabel Rebecca Beaston Sober. They had three other children, a girl and two boys.[20] Like thousands of other people, the Sober family came to Indian Territory in 1889 in search of a better life and settled in Oklahoma City. Morris worked as a carpenter, while Isabel cooked for railroad men.

Gertrude worked at several different jobs. She clerked in a store, taught school, and, after the family got homesteads in different areas, tried her skills at farming.[21] Her 160-acre plot lay in Roger Mills County near Sweetwater. For a time, she existed on such roughage as kafir bread and whatever she could muster from nature's table. That homesteading failure led to office work and finally to her mining venture.[22]

After she was widowed, Gertrude went to Norman and enrolled at the University of Oklahoma. She kept boarders to support herself. In 1933, at age sixty-four, she earned a degree in geology. But who in those days would hire a sixty-four-year-old woman geologist?[23] The remainder of her working years, she managed apartments in Oklahoma City and invested in oil and a citrus farm in Texas.

Gertrude died in a nursing home in Oklahoma City and was buried in Jamison Cemetery, Lincoln County. In 1988 she was posthumously inducted into the Miners' Hall of Fame in Leadville, Colorado, the only woman in it.

DR. INEZ BAUCUM
(1915-   )
"Second Mother" to Multitudes

More than half a century as a dedicated social and child welfare worker and a university professor —that is a short *vita* of Dr. Inez Baucum. Oklahoma born and raised, Inez got her inspiration to serve unfortunate humanity from her own youth as an orphan and a book she read in the eighth grade. It was titled *Slums of New York*.[24] This influence increased through high school and into the deep, dark days of the Dust Bowl and the Great Depression.

She got a job working for her room and board at Ada, Oklahoma, and went to enroll in East Central State Teachers College (now University). "I want to major in something," she told the dean, "that will help me help other people."[25] He directed her to social work, a new addition to the curriculum in those days. She settled in to a lifetime of study and service to others.

After three years at East Central, she transferred to the University of Oklahoma at Norman. She worked part time as a secretary and graduated in

Dr. Inez Baucum stands at the Great Wall of China. The trip was given at her retirement in appreciation for her life's work with children. (Courtesy Dr. Inez Baucum)

1939 with a B.A. degree in Social Work.[26] Her first full-time job was in the Public Assistance Division of the Department of Public Welfare at Sayre, Oklahoma. Her work was so satisfactory the director asked if she would like to change to Child Welfare and do graduate study at Tulane or Columbia.[27] "I thought a moment," Inez said. "I knew nothing about either place, but Tulane sounded romantic and a bit mystical. Then I said 'Yes. Tulane.' I got a scholarship from the National Children's Bureau in Washington, D.C."

Inez laughed. She often laughed at her youthful naiveté, which sparked much of her humor and her popularity as a speaker. "It was then," she continued, "I learned Tulane University was in New Orleans, Louisiana. I had never been very far from home, but I wasn't about to let that spoil a wonderful opportunity."

That experience was a step up in her life of service. When she returned from Tulane, she reported to Ada, Oklahoma, as a child welfare worker. That was a two-year stint after which she moved to Kay County. There she covered Ponca City, Blackwell, and Tonkawa.[28]

In the late 1940s Inez took time off from work to earn a master's degree from the School of Social Administration at the University of Chicago on a scholarship. That resulted in an advancement to child welfare consultant in Norman. Next she went to Duncan where she covered twenty-three Southwest Oklahoma counties and supervised five workers.[29]

While at Duncan, Inez was approached by officials of a church group in Lubbock, Texas, to come there and establish an adoption and foster care agency for the Children's Home of Lubbock.[30] The home was sponsored by the Broadway Church of Christ in Lubbock. Inez would be the first social worker for that religious group. It was not a difficult decision to make. Inez had worked for the Public Welfare Department of her home state for sixteen years. She had advanced steadily and was receiving a better salary than she would receive at the church home. But money was not her idol. Her best service to God and humanity was. She made the change in 1955.[31]

For twenty-five years Inez drove, often alone, over Texas and its neighboring states to investigate and collect children who needed care: orphans, the homeless, those who were dependent, neglected, and abused. She interviewed prospective adoptive and foster parents, consulted judges and probation officers, and placed children accordingly. Many times she traveled day and night.[32]

One couple, who adopted a child through her, told of such an occasion. "After we got Kim," the mother said, "Inez came to see how we were getting along. It was ten o'clock in the evening when she started to leave. We asked her to spend the night. She said she couldn't. She had to go to work in the morning."[33]

The father joined the conversation. "I asked what she would do if she had a flat or other car trouble," he said, "out there on the road alone. She said she'd cross that bridge when she came to it, then drove off into the night. It was more than two hundred miles back to Lubbock."

During her quarter of a century at the home, Inez was instrumental in arranging the adoption of six hundred children into private homes. She assisted thousands of others in getting foster care and many other necessities of life. They call her "Second Mother."[34] While still working at the Children's Home, Inez began teaching a class in the Social Services Department at Lubbock Christian College (now University). After she retired from the home, she became an assistant professor. As she grew older, the number of her classes was reduced. She retired in 1991.[35]

Throughout both professions Inez was involved in volunteer work. She conducted workshops and seminars and spoke at educational institutions, civic clubs, the League of Women Voters, and numerous other organizations. She served on commissions, boards, and committees. In addition she did post-graduate work at Pepperdine University in California and wrote poetry and prose for religious and secular publications.[36] But her life was not all work, which she seemed to enjoy thoroughly. She traveled in the United States and to distant lands. In 1960 she was a Texas delegate to the White House Conference on Children and Youth. Inez visited nine countries in Europe on one trip and traveled through the Holy Land on another. Next she went to Russia, Sweden and Denmark.[37]

When Inez retired from the Children's Home, she was given a trip to China. The Forbidden City in Beijing (Peking) and the Great Wall on the border of Mongolia were impressive and memorable sights, but one incident stirred a bit of trauma.[38] "While on another sightseeing trip," Inez recalled, "I reached in my pocket to see if my passport was intact. To my horror it was missing! I told Norvel Young, our director," Inez continued, "and he turned white. I told George Bailey, our guide, and he turned white. We couldn't believe it. That meant all kinds of problems. We were on the verge of despair."

As the three gazed at one another, a six-foot, four-inch-tall man raised an object and shouted, "Did anyone lose this passport?"

Inez sighed, then chuckled. "That was a time for rejoicing," she said, "believe me. My pocket had ripped and the passport had slipped to the floor."

As both a pleasure and service, Inez spent two weeks helping with the "River of Life Exhibit" at the World's Fair in New Orleans in 1984. It was sponsored by the Churches of Christ.[39]

Her continued contributions resulted in continued awards and honors. For her work with the Smithlawn Maternity Home for unfortunate girls in Lubbock she had a residence named for her—the "Inez Baucum Cottage."[40] For her contribution to the city, such as the Chamber of Commerce, the mayor of Lubbock declared an "Inez Baucum Day." Lubbock Christian University awarded her an honorary Doctor of Laws degree.[41] She was listed in

Who's Who in the South and Southwest. The Texas Chapter of the National Association of Social Workers presented her the "Lifetime Achievement Award."

Her many other honors include 20th Century Christian's "Century Woman of the Year" and "Outstanding Educator of America." Even after she retired from the University, she continued getting awards. In 1992 she was honored as "Friend of the Child" from the Children's Home of Lubbock.[42]

A brief glimpse of how all this came together follows. The daughter of the late David R. and Hattie Conyers Baucum, Inez grew up the middle child of three. That was usually considered unlucky or ill-fated, but she never considered it so. Her brother Malcolm was five when their father, a merchant, died in 1919. Inez was four and her sister Gladys was sixteen months.[43]

In those days few people carried life insurance, and not many women were considered for professional work. To support her children, Mother Hattie resorted to domestic work, home nursing, clerking in stores, washing, and even picking cotton.[44] She taught the children well, took them to church, and, like the village blacksmith, sat among them. Inez recalls her childhood with endearment and humor. One incident involved a very close friend, Exa Chaffin Webb. "We wanted to go to the fortune-teller," Inez told the local historical society, "but didn't know how we could do it. I had a nickel, but Exa had no money at all and I wouldn't go without her. Finally I said, 'Let's try anyway.'"[45]

"We went to her house and I ventured up to the door to knock," Inez laughed. "When she came out, I asked if she would tell both our fortunes for a nickel.

Dr. Inez Baucum discusses some of the children for whom she found homes. (Courtesy Dr. Inez Baucum)

The woman glared at us a moment. I told her a nickel was all we had. Her eyes twinkled and she said, 'Yes. Come on in.' We did and I felt a bit smarter and more grown-up by the things she told us."

Inez never said what the woman told her, but if she said "marriage was in the coffee grounds," she was wrong. Fate seemed to determine her future otherwise. During World War II Inez became engaged to Alfred Crow of Ada, but Uncle Sam called him into service during an emergency. He never came back. His supreme sacrifice was made in Italy on October 10, 1944. His body was returned to Ada for burial.[46] As to her siblings, Malcolm became a lawyer, but died young. Gladys worked for the municipality of Oklahoma City until she retired. Both married and had children.

Through all those years Inez had kept the Baucum home in Sulphur. Although wracked with age, it remains her summer haven. "I love this old house," she said, "and want it left as it is."[47] While in Sulphur, she renews childhood friendships and participates in church and high school alumni reunions. Back in Lubbock she remains on boards and committees, is Professor Emeritus Designate at Lubbock Christian University, and teaches a Bible class at Broadway Church of Christ for business and professional women. Her wit and wisdom continue to keep her a popular speaker.[48]

VESTA ARMSTRONG MAUCK
(1922-   )
Another Exciting Life at Age Sixty

It took Vesta Armstrong Mauck three children, five grandchildren, and twelve years, but she made it. In February 1982 at age sixty, Vesta, of El Dorado Hills, California, received her license as a marriage, family, and child counselor. And she got a job![49]

Vesta worked forty hours a week for the non-profit county agency, New Morning, at Placerville, twenty miles from her home. During those forty work hours, she spent two days in the office where she counseled children and/or parents on their problems. Three days each week she went to one of the high schools to confer with students, referred to her by teachers.[50] Ten days a month she was on "Crisis Call" twenty-four hours a day. New Morning dealt with runaway children in the county; thus Vesta answered the summons day or night. Generally it was for children picked up by the police. Vesta's

assignment was to find approved shelter for the youngsters.[51]

Most all of Vesta's clients were adolescents. "It was amazing," she said, "how helpful it seemed to them to have someone who would listen to their side of the story. I tried to make them aware," she continued, "of how they had played into their own problems—what their process was in dealing with others. Was it working? If not, did they want to change it? We discussed alternatives."[52]

In addition to her work at New Morning, Vesta did private practice, seeing clients in the evening. Also, she provided counseling for those who planned to be married by the priest at the church she attended.[53] "This was a special joy," Vesta said, "a feeling I was helping prevent problems rather than having to deal with them after the fact."

Vesta's most traumatic experience was equally traumatic for her client. It was her first time to deal with such a problem. "It involved a fourteen-year-old girl," she said, her brown eyes filled with memories, "who had been sexually abused by her father. It had lasted seven years. It took a lot of counseling before her wounds began to heal."[54]

Why did Vesta begin a career so late in life when

Below: Vesta Armstrong Mauck looks up from her work in her office in California. She now is a marriage, family, and child counselor. (Courtesy Vesta Armstrong Mauck)

most people she knew, including her husband, had retired or were on the verge of doing so? "It had always been in the back of my mind," she said, smiling. "I had a feeling I wasn't living up to my potential. Furthermore, our children were becoming autonomous and independent. I needed a substitute, and I didn't want just a job. It became evident I'd have to complete my education to do something meaningful."[55]

Why did she choose counseling? "People had often brought their problems to me," she explained, "and all I could do was listen, feel with them and be frustrated. I had no tools or techniques to help them. Counseling provided these and enabled me to be helpful." Vesta sat a little taller and her face glowed. "It was exciting to me."

What did her husband and others think about the idea? "Initially," she chuckled, "Ed resented my interest in it. Once he said, 'I don't want to hear about your school experiences.' It seemed threatening to him. Then pride in my accomplishments seemed to have taken over. He became supportive. A few," Vesta continued with a quizzical lean to her head, "seemed to envy my energy and enthusiasm. Others couldn't understand my working when I didn't have to."[56]

A native of Shawnee, Oklahoma, Vesta attended schools in Konawa and Guthrie, where she graduated. From there she went to Oklahoma State University at Stillwater three semesters, from 1939 through 1941. World War II wrought many changes. Vesta's parents, Fred and Gertrude Simpson, moved to another oil field job at Great Bend, Kansas. Vesta joined them. She worked as a receptionist in a doctor's office until she married Second Lieutenant Leon Edwin Mauck. The ceremony was in Albuquerque, New Mexico.[57] Lieutenant Mauck's training led the couple to Hopkinsville, Kentucky, then military service took him with the 12th Armored Division to Europe. Vesta returned to her former job in Kansas for the duration.

When her husband returned, he was a captain. After his discharge, the couple went into business in Concordia, Kansas, for a short time, then he switched to Civil Service.[58] Captain Mauck's position as management analyst for the United States Air Force took the family to Topeka. From there they went to San Bernardino, California, then to Sacramento. It was there they bought a home in El Dorado Hills where they live today (1993).

During those years the couple had three chil-

At age sixty Vesta Armstrong Mauck graduated from college with her son, Ronnie Mauck. Born and raised in Oklahoma, Vesta now lives in California. Ronnie is a city planner in Porterville, California. (Courtesy Vesta Armstrong Mauck)

dren: Ronald, Marcia, and Jana. When Ronald was a baby in Kansas, it became necessary for Vesta to go to work.[59] "The guilt I felt at leaving him with a sitter," she said, "was overwhelming. I quit as soon as possible. I loved the job, but felt guilty about it. Too, I entertained the logic a wife and mother shouldn't enjoy a job away from home. So," Vesta chuckled, "in the twenty-eight years I was married before I returned to college, I worked only one and a half years."

By 1970 Vesta was ready for a change. Ronald and Marcia were married and had children. Jana was eleven and helpful. Vesta enrolled in college.[60] "While I earned a bachelor's degree in Social Services," she said, "I did field work for Sacramento County as liaison person between the County Children's Service Office and the schools. I dealt with children who had excessive absenteeism, and helped their families solve problems contributing to this condition."

Vesta graduated from California State University at Sacramento with her son Ronald. They celebrated, then she went for a graduate degree in counseling. "They gave me a special assignment," Vesta said, "of field work at the Family Counseling Center in the San Juan School District at Carmichael,

California. I worked with individuals and families who were experiencing a broad spectrum of problems."

After receiving a master's degree, Vesta continued working on a part-time basis until she earned her State Pupil Personnel Credentials. That was in 1980.[61] "Suddenly," she said, "I felt a need to do more. To reach my ultimate goal, the California Marriage, Family, and Child Counseling License, I had to log three thousand hours of supervised counseling and pass stiff written and oral examinations. They were given by the state. Only six states require such exams. I completed mine in February of 1982." That was Vesta's birth month.

Meanwhile she began looking for a full-time job. "I was interviewed," she said, "by the director of New Morning and chosen over a number of applicants. Most of them were twenty-five to thirty-five years younger than I.[62] It was then," she continued, "I realized the fear no one would hire a gray-haired lady was unfounded. In the profession I had chosen, maturation and experience in living seemed to have been assets."

Does Vesta think all the time and money spent preparing for her belated profession were worth the sacrifice? "A definite yes," she declared quickly. "Best time, best energy, and best money I ever spent were on the education. It prepared me for this fulfilling and gratifying work.

"I'm a lucky person," she continued. "I've enjoyed each phase of my life. I very much liked the roles of daughter, wife, mother, grandmother, student. Each had its rewards and was sufficient at the time. And now, confining my counseling to office work only, it is the crème de la crème of all roles and all ages put together."[63]

****

Such women help inspire others to write, especially to write biography and history. Three women, who have excelled in this genre, are featured in this last chapter. One of them made history.

Chapter 13
HISTORIANS-ACTIVISTS

DR. ANGIE DEBO
(1890-1988)
Historian of Controversy—Historian of Note

"When I finished the manuscript for *And Still the Waters Run* in 1936," Dr. Angie Debo said, "the University of Oklahoma Press would not touch it. Those in charge said it involved too many people in high places at that time."[1] Dr. Angie was speaking at a meeting of Oklahoma Press Women at Oklahoma State University in Stillwater. That was in 1977. The book, *And Still the Waters Run*, detailed and authenticated its subtitle, "The Betrayal of the Five Civilized Tribes."

"The University Press," Dr. Angie continued her talk, "had published my first book, *The Rise and Fall of the Choctaw Republic*. It was a revision of my dissertation for a Ph.D. in history from O.U., so I thought it would take this one. Naturally, I was disappointed. Dejected. After further negotiations, however, Princeton University Press in New Jersey published *And Still the Waters Run* in 1940."[2]

With a serious look on her scrubbed, aging face, Dr. Angie continued to tell what her research uncovered. She named people her audience knew by reputation, some personally, who cheated and deceived unsuspecting Indians. They included politicians, lawyers, businessmen. And some of them were still considered "heroes."[3]

Another of Dr. Angie's controversial books was *Geronimo, the Man, His Time, His Place*. That Apache, whose mother christened him a tribal name meaning "One Who Yawns," had always been depicted as a depraved chief and warrior roaming the Southwest and ravaging white people like an animal.[4] Dr. Angie debunked that image to a great extent. She reported both sides of the story. Her information was based on research at Lawton's Museum of the Great Plains, Fort Sill's museum, and elsewhere. Geronimo was not a chief, but a medicine man and prophet.

He suffered much, including the loss of his family at the hands of encroaching whites and soldiers on the chase. He fought back, surrendered, was incarcerated in Florida, and finally returned to Fort Sill as a prisoner of war.[5] Geronimo lived on the reservation, not in the guardhouse. He joined the Dutch Reformed Church and died of pneumonia in 1909.[6]

Among Dr. Angie's other six books were *A History of the Indian Tribes of the United States, Prairie City, Tulsa, The Road to Disappearance—a History of the Creek Indians, Footloose and Fancy Free*, and *The Five Civilized Tribes*. She did much more writing, including editing other books.[7]

Dr. Angie was the daughter of Edward P. and Lisa Debo. She was born in Beattie, Kansas, about 1890. Some nine years later, she came to Oklahoma Territory in a covered wagon with her parents and a younger brother. The family settled at the frontier town of Marshall, north of Oklahoma City about halfway between Stillwater and Enid.[8]

At age sixteen, young Angie began teaching in

Below: Never faltering, Dr. Angie Debo, noted historian of Marshall, told it as it was. (Courtesy Western History Collections, the University of Oklahoma)

rural schools. When Marshall established a high school, she quit teaching and enrolled. After graduating, she finished college and went to the University of Chicago to earn a master's degree. Having a thirst for knowledge and integrity, Angie entered the University of Oklahoma, where she received a doctor's degree in history.[9]

It was Depression days. Jobs were difficult to find. Besides, most of the historians were men. Like millions of others, Dr. Angie had some lean days. Almost skeletal. But she finally landed a job. One branch of the WPA (Works Progress Administration) used writers. They traveled throughout the country, interviewing "Old Timers" for historic information. Dr. Angie became editor of the project and supervised some forty reporters. The result was a series of bound and indexed books of personalized stories titled "Oklahoma Pioneer Indian History." The books are preserved in the Oklahoma Historical Society building in Oklahoma City. They are a boon to historical researchers.[10]

Dr. Angie received numerous awards and honors for her work, the last of which was a TV feature on David McCullough's series, "The American Experience." It aired on PBS (Public Broadcasting System) in 1989 and 1990. The film was based to an extent on the book, *And Still the Waters Run*. The feature was titled "Indians, Outlaws and Angie Debo."[11]

Instrumental in the film were Dr. Glenna Matthews and Gloria Valencia-Weber of Oklahoma State University. They made an earlier tape of Dr. Angie and were so deeply impressed by her story, they passed the information on to the Institute for Research in History in New York City.[12]

A big triumph for Dr. Angie's work was in 1984 when the University of Oklahoma Press arranged with Princeton to publish her most controversial book, *And Still the Waters Run*, in paperback. That was forty-four years after the same press had rejected it.[13]

Dr. Angie never married. She spent most of her life in the small town of Marshall, studying, writing, lecturing, and doing church work. She was revered by all who knew her.

****

Oklahoma has produced other notable and most deserving women historians. Among them are Muriel Wright, Zoe Tilghman, and Carolyn Foreman.

BERENICE LLOYD JACKSON
(1908-   )
Panhandle Historian of Note

Why would the news media from the *Chicago Tribune*, the American Broadcasting Company and the British Broadcasting Corporation send reporters to Woodward, Oklahoma? And why would the schools in England use tapes made there?[14] The answer is because residents of that area attracted international attention to their accomplishments. The stimulus for that accomplishment was Berenice Lloyd Jackson.[15]

Berenice, a native of Beaver County in the Panhandle, was somewhat of an authority on the history of the area. Her parents Landom ("Dick") and Clara Childress Lloyd came there from Missouri when all the Panhandle was called Beaver County, Oklahoma Territory.[16] Berenice received her elementary education in a one-room school, graduated from Beaver (city) High School, then enrolled in Panhandle A and M College at Goodwell. Her joint major was English and history.

A severe drought brought widespread financial trouble, so Berenice decided to teach. She passed the teachers' examination and landed a position teaching grades one through four in a two-room school. Love between her and the students was mutual.[17] That love extended to a young man, Brice Jackson, and they married in 1930. That union terminated her public school teaching career. Depression added to drought brought such poverty to the country that school authorities made the decision not to hire married women.

Brice and Berenice lived on the quarter section of land he owned at the time they married. The first ten years were a struggle. The Great Depression and dust storms were more than many people could take, so they abandoned the area and headed west. But the two young Jacksons stuck with it and came out victors.[18] During that period they had a son, John Lloyd Jackson. He became a joy and comfort to them. Berenice began offering private piano lessons, charging twenty-five cents for a thirty-minute session. Not until 1972 did she raise the price of her lessons to $1.25. Following the Depression and World War II, the economy improved, so the Jacksons could add 540 more acres to their homestead. They lived there fifty-four years.[19]

In 1968 the home economist, Mary Lou Sadler, appointed Berenice chairman of the newly formed

Reporters from the British Broadcasting Corporation traveled to Woodward to interview Berenice Lloyd Jackson. She is shown here delivering a story to her local newspaper. (Courtesy Berenice Lloyd Jackson)

Fine Arts Division of the Homemakers Club. First on the agenda was to write a county history. The group organized the county into clubs and began their promotion. That started a "prairie fire" that could not be stopped. Never had a whole county become so interested as Beaver County people were to get that history underway. Berenice drove eighty-six miles a day for three years to collect material for two volumes. The first was composed of 672 pages of family histories. It came off the press in the spring of 1970. The next year Volume II was released. Numbering 608 pages, it contained the actual history of Beaver County.[20]

During this period the Beaver County Historical Society was organized, and Berenice was elected president. She appeared on the "Danny's Day" program from Oklahoma City and five times on Channel 6 from Ensign, Kansas, to advertise the history books. In recognition of Berenice's tireless work on this project, the Beaver Chapter of the national organization of Jaycees presented her with their Outstanding Citizenry Award. This was in 1972.

It was through her efforts that markers were placed at thirty-nine ghost towns in Beaver County. She realized that those towns were important to the early pioneers and that their history needed to be preserved. Berenice did not stop there. R.A. Young, president of Oklahoma Heritage Association, said,[21]

> Berenice Jackson, serving as chairman of the History-Heritage committee of Red Carpet Country, representing nineteen counties in Northwest Oklahoma, has been one of the most dynamic forces in historical preservation in our state. She personally led the efforts three years ago to bring about the publication of a Beaver County history.
>
> Today she is the force behind an effort to bring about production of histories throughout Northwest Oklahoma. In addition Mrs. Jackson is leading an oral history project and an effort to organize high school heritage clubs throughout Red Carpet Country.
>
> In recognition of these efforts, the Oklahoma Heritage Association is proud to present this Award of Special Merit to Mrs. Berenice Jackson of Beaver County, Oklahoma.[22]

The date was January 18, 1974.

Later Berenice was honored again when the Oklahoma Heritage Association presented her the Stanley Draper Award. The next year she was elected to the Board of Directors of the Oklahoma Historical Society. She served on six different committees, but retired when her husband became seriously ill.

After the Beaver County histories were published, Berenice saw the need to write a history of the entire Panhandle. She and Brice began interviewing residents and researching in libraries, museums and other such places. They went to Canyon, Texas; Norman, and Oklahoma City, Oklahoma; Denver, Colorado; and several places in New Mexico.[23] As Berenice said, "Dinosaurs didn't stop at state lines in their era of time."

In 1982, fifteen hundred copies of *Man and the Oklahoma Panhandle* came off the press. They sold out the first year, and five hundred more copies were printed. All those will soon be gone. *Man and the Oklahoma Panhandle* is a beautiful and well-written production. Organized in three sections, it covers the geology, archaeology, and history from earliest times to Statehood in 1907.

In 1987 Berenice's name was sent to the state office as a participant in President Ronald Reagan's program, "Take Pride in America." More than five hundred were entered. Berenice was among the twenty-five semifinalists. She and her daughter-in-law, Paula Jackson, attended the programs in Washington, D.C., after which they visited many interesting places in the capital city.[24]

Due to her efforts, Beaver County now has two structures on the National Register of Historic Places: the Presbyterian Church and the James Lane sod house. And another honor to Berenice—she is listed in the book, *Personalities of the South*. She has been interviewed many times for information on the Dust Bowl days—once by a reporter from the *Chicago Tribune*. The story was syndicated, a fact that led to ABC's sending Dan Noyes to Woodward to interview Berenice. His tape was aired a week later on "Good Morning America."[25] A chain reaction brought BBC's Edwina Vardley to Woodward to interview Berenice and several others relative to the Dust Bowl days. This tape was used in the schools of England.

Berenice lost her son in 1986 and her husband in 1988. She lives alone in Woodward and still does interviews. She continues to do volunteer work in museums and to enjoy her grandchildren, her church, her clubs and her numerous friends.

(Information provided by Berenice Jackson and her friends.)

CLARA SHEPARD LUPER
A Nonviolent Fighter

Arrested twenty-six times, threatened with a pan of dangerous chemicals, almost run over by a motorist, cursed, insulted, spat upon for years, Clara Shepard Luper endured all those things and more. But she pressed on without violence.[26] "For some reason," she said, "I believed God sent us (black activists) here to make the experiment of democracy work." She set out in the mid-1900s to do just that.

During Negro History Week in 1957, Clara presented a play, *Brother President*, with her history students at Dunjee High School in Spencer, Oklahoma. The play was based on the story of Martin Luther King's struggle to eliminate segregation in Montgomery, Alabama. Clara received more requests for the play.[27] Herbert Wright, national youth director of the National Association for the Advancement for Colored People, was in the audience during a second presentation, which was in the East Sixth Street Christian Church, Oklahoma City. He asked Clara to take the cast to New York City and present the play at the "Rally to Salute the Young Freedom Fighters."

Nonviolent activist Clara Shepard Luper made history as one of Martin Luther King's supporters. Speaking to the Mid-Oklahoma Writers in March 1993 at Rose State College in Midwest City, Clara told of her people's struggle for equality. Betty Personnette is taping the presentation. (Taken by the author)

The two agreed that the students would raise money for their own transportation and that Wright would provide their lodging and food. Some of the students had never been out of Oklahoma, but they all got a slice of integrated society—in hotels, restaurants, and public facilities. These experiences sharpened their determination to fight for "freedom."[28]

Back in Oklahoma the students and Clara spent eighteen months planning their strategy. They contacted officials and property owners with proposals to repeal city ordinances and state laws which bound them to segregation. They contacted church leaders and many others to help. The activists faced "stone walls."[29] With Clara as their official NAACP Youth Council advisor, the members pledged nonviolence, honesty, and love for their enemies. Also to "give the white man a way out...let him participate in victory when it comes." Then came action.

Their first target was Katz Drug Store in downtown Oklahoma City. They walked in and sat at the all-white counter.[30]

"What do you all want?" a waitress barked.

"We'd like thirteen Cokes, please," one of the girls said.

"You can have them to go," the waitress answered.

"We'll drink them here," the girl said and laid a five-dollar bill on the counter.

The waitress called the manager. He hurried to Clara, chastised her, and ordered: "Take these children out this moment!"

"Thirteen Cokes, please," she answered.

The manager called the police. They came, along with members of the press. A cameraman was "thrown out." Whites at the counter left food and drink to "empty their hate at the group."

"Move, you black SOB," one of them spat at Clara.[31]

Clara took a copy of Martin Luther King's *Non-Violent Plans* from her purse and began to read. It was lengthy. By the time she finished, some black cooks and janitors entered the drug store. Yes, Clara mused to herself, the blacks could cook for and clean up after the whites, but they were not good enough to eat at the same place. The NAACP group decided to leave, but they had passed their first test with calmness. When Clara arrived home, she faced criticism from some of her own race. On the other hand, she also received enough encouragement to revitalize her and the movement.[32]

Two days later Katz announced that thirty-eight of the company's outlets in Missouri, Oklahoma, Kansas, and Iowa "would serve all people, regardless of race, creed or color."

Veazey's Drug Store was the youth group's second target. The manager met them with "Welcome." Surprised, but pleased, they ordered soft drinks, paid, then tipped the waitress and left. At the group's third place, S.H. Kress, the manager welcomed them to an empty space. He said they could stand up and eat. The workers had removed all chairs and tables. The young people left and went to John A. Brown's. One of the most classic stores in the country, Brown's had a luncheonette in the basement.[33]

Clara had traded in that department store for years. She even had a charge account there. So did many other blacks, but on August 22, 1958, no one would have believed it. Clerks, who had always met her with a smile, now stood frozen to the floor.

One made a face, while another harassed the group. Clara thought she and her group were in a lion's den. Her companion thought they were "in hell." The group began to sing, "Joshua fought the Battle of Jericho..., and the walls came tumbling down."[34]

They were not served in the luncheonette, but John A. Brown's became the "Bunker Hill of the sit-in movement." Day in and day out protestors went to Brown's. "The day before Halloween, the youths stayed up until 3:00 a.m. making white masks for 150 activists," mostly young people. Ghostly in those masks, the group entered Brown's later in the day and approached the guard in the basement. "My face is white," they chanted. "May I eat today? I'm ready to pay...."[35] The irony did not phase the storekeepers, but the activists continued.

Halloween 1963 came "and still no food." The group rented a devil's costume and one of the members wore it to Brown's, then to Anna Maud's Cafeteria, which also was segregated. The "devil" danced around and called for his angels, designating the managers. No visible results were forthcoming, but the activists continued. Several whites and many NAACP members from out of state strengthened the pressure. Finally, Mrs. John A. Brown called for Clara (Mr. Brown had been deceased for some time).[36]

With some hesitance, Clara answered the call and agreed to a meeting. It turned out to be emotional. They wept together and became good friends. Mrs. Brown's previous reasoning had been: "What will my white customers think? I'll lose money."

In addition to sit-ins, stand-ins, boycotts, and demonstrations the NAACP Youth Council members attended conferences and marches around the country. They received awards for their participation. In 1957 they were involved in the push for fair housing. Among the things they did in 1968 was establish a Freedom Center. They purchased an old filling station and restored it for a place to meet and keep supplies. The same year someone called Clara to warn her that it was being bombed, and it was. Some city officials awoke and helped her start another one.[37]

In 1969 a major involvement was a protest at Lawton. Black soldiers at Fort Sill, who had fought and lost their buddies in Viet Nam, could not swim in the pool at Doe Doe Amusement Park. They complained. The Oklahoma City youths and Clara made four marches and drives to that city. The first time, the manager ordered them out of the park. "Fist fights followed," but stopped short of serious problems. The activists began singing,[38] "He's got the whole world in his hand, He's got old Ben Hutchins..., then Mayor Gilley..., the city council...." The situation remained status quo.

A week later the young people with more adults joined activists of Lawton at Doe Doe Park. Clara, Senator Melvin Porter, a white Catholic priest from Lawton, and seven young people were jailed. Ten children, ages five to thirteen, were placed in the Juvenile Ward.[39] Lawton officials let Clara out to take the children home, and Dr. Owens paid the twenty-dollar fines. The last trip was a foot and soul bruiser. People joined their march-drive all along the way. Next day at the park "Hutchins was ready to negotiate." Mayor Gilley came to pledge that the recently created Human Rights Commission would take up the proposed ordinance to eliminate discrimination in all public places.[40]

The group's next move was to appoint a committee to study and recommend that Oklahoma City's manager "increase minorities in its employment forces." Clara headed that committee. She advocated a strike and landed in jail. Senator Porter bailed her out.[41] More marches, more visits and calls to officials, additional arrests, one of which included black State Representative Hannah Atkins. Oklahoma City's chief of police took Clara's press pass and never returned it. Top members of the NAACP arrived in Oklahoma City. After more picketing, threats, marches and mayhem, city officials finally agreed to talk and eventually yield to the sanitation workers' demands.[42]

On another bright day, members burned the mortgage of the NAACP's new Freedom Center.[43]

What gave Clara Shepard Luper such stamina to carry on so many years? Her background might answer that question. Born in Okfuskee County to Mr. and Mrs. Ezell Shepard, she grew up and attended public schools in Hoffman.[44] Her father, a World War I veteran, was a farmer. Her mother washed and ironed for people. One woman required her to pick up the clothes at the back door. "My parents taught me to board the bus," Clara said, "and go to the back. I asked why, but Mother said, 'Shut up.' Father was a dreamer. He told me some day I would be able to board a bus and sit anywhere I chose. Neither was very well educated, but they had a master's degree in honesty.[45]

"One day at school," Clara continued, "the teacher asked what fathers did. I didn't know, so that evening I asked Father. He said, 'Tell them I'm a pilot. I pile dirt here, and I pile dirt there.' They both believed education was the way out for us. We had to study and memorize poems and verses from the Bible."[46]

Clara graduated from Langston University and was the first black student to enroll in the History Department at the University of Oklahoma. She had to sit behind a partition, but she tested above all the others in that department. She earned a master's degree, did graduate study at Oklahoma City University, and traveled "for an education." She taught history and public relations at Dunjee High School in Spencer and at John Marshall and Classen High Schools in Oklahoma City. Most of her work with the NAACP Youth Council and others was done during weekends and summers.[47]

Clara made a race for the State Senate, but lost. Another challenge was a debate with the Grand Dragon of the Ku Klux Klan. She did not lose that.[48] "I'm happy," she began, "to debate my white brother...."

Her opponent exploded: "I want you to understand I'm not your brother...." That was all she needed.

Clara won 150 awards and citations for her work with young people, three of whom were her own: Marilyn, Calvin, and Chelle Marie Luper. She is very proud of them and all the rest of her relatives.[49]

"Yes," she said, "I have seen changes unbelievable in my lifetime. Twenty-three years after the sit-ins began, my family held a reunion in a hotel in downtown Oklahoma City."[50] Clara beamed. She did not look near the age she had to be to have stood up to her punishment during the Civil Rights Movement.

EPILOGUE

So where do modern women enter the issue? Certainly they have made distinguished contributions. They have brought attention to their sex, made progress on equality, and helped raise the income of women. It seems assured they will accomplish more, but....

They need to recognize the fact that their older sisters cut the trail through thorns and thistles, thus decreasing the scratches and abrasions they will suffer along their way.

ENDNOTES

Chapter 1:

[1]Byron Biles, *How Green Was My Valley, a History of the Biles Family* (N.p., n.d.), 14.

[2]*Ibid.*

[3]*Ibid.*, 615.

[4]*Ibid.*

[5]*Ibid.*, 616.

[6]*Ibid.*

[7]*Ibid.*

[8]Ruby Biles Wilson, granddaughter, letter to author, 1991.

[9]Ellen Hermann Douthitt, Diary, 1889-1910.

[10]*Ibid.*

[11]Jeff and Reba Jennings, grandchildren, interview with author, 1992.

[12]Ellen Hermann Douthitt, Diary, 1889-1910.

[13]*Ibid.*

[14]*Ibid.*

[15]*Ibid.*

[16]Jeff and Reba Jennings, grandchildren, interview with author, 1992.

[17]*Ibid.*

[18]Ellen Hermann Douthitt, Diary, 1889-1910.

[19]*Ibid.*; Writers' Program of the Work Projects Administration of the State of Oklahoma, *The WPA Guide to 1930s Oklahoma* (Lawrence: University Press of Kansas, 1986), 371.

[20]Jeff and Reba Jennings, interview with author, 1992.

[21]Ellen Hermann Douthitt, Diary, 1889-1910.

[22]*Ibid.*

[23]Jeff and Reba Jennings, interview with author, 1992.

[24]*Ibid.*; Ellen Hermann Douthitt, Diary, 1889-1910.

[25]*Ibid.*

[26]Jeff and Reba Jennings, interview with author, 1992.

[27]*Ibid.*

[28]*Ibid.*

[29]Harriet Patrick Gilstrap, "Memories of a Pioneer Teacher," *Chronicles of Oklahoma* (XXXVIII), 24.

[30]*Ibid.*

[31]*Ibid.*

[32]*Ibid.*, 25.

[33]*Ibid.*

[34]*Ibid.*

[35]*Ibid.*

[36]*Ibid.*, 26.

[37]*Ibid.*, 27.

[38]*Ibid.*, 28.

[39]*Ibid.*

[40]*Ibid.*, 20.

[41]*Ibid.*, 21.

[42]*Ibid.*

[43]*Ibid.*

[44]*Ibid.*, 22.

[45]*Ibid.*

[46]*Ibid.*

[47]Colonel Charles Mooney, *Localized History of Pottawatomie County, Oklahoma to 1907* (1971), 53.

[48]Southwest Oklahoma Genealogical Society, *Comanche County History*, 21.

[49]*Ibid.*, 19.

[50]*Ibid.*

[51]*Ibid.*

[52]*Ibid.*, 21; Audrey Adams Routh, *Prairie Lore* (Southwest Oklahoma Historical Society, Autumn, 1986), 38.

[53]Kenny L. Brown, "The Land Lottery of 1901," *Prairie Lore* (Southwest Oklahoma Historical Society, July, 1979), 10.

[54]Southwest Oklahoma Genealogical Society, *Comanche County History*, 20.

[55]Kenny L. Brown, "The Land Lottery of 1901," *Prairie Lore* (Southwest Oklahoma Historical Society, July, 1979), 11.

[56]Southwest Oklahoma Genealogical Society, *Comanche County History*, 23.

[57]*Ibid.*, 25.

[58]*Ibid.*, 23-24.

[59]*Ibid.*, 26.

[60]*Ibid.*, 27.

[61]*Ibid.*, 28.

[62]*Ibid.*, p132-133.

[63]*Ibid.*, 407.

Chapter 2:

[1]Sippia Paul Hull, "Reminiscences of Mrs. Sippia Hull," July 2, 1929 (Archives, Pauls Valley Memorial Library); also in Arbuckle Historical Societies of Davis and Sulphur, "Reminiscences of Mrs. Sippia Hull," *Murray County History* (II, PhotoGraphics, 1988), 21.

[2]*Ibid.*

[3]*Ibid.*; Gary Schilling, "Fort Arbuckle," Opal Hartsell Brown, *Murray County* (Wichita Falls: Nortex Press, 1977), 8.

[4]Sippia Paul Hull, "Reminiscences of Mrs. Sippia Hull," July 2, 1929 (Archives, Pauls Valley Memorial Library); also in Arbuckle Historical Societies of Davis and Sulphur, "Reminiscences of Mrs. Sippia Hull," *Murray County History* (II), 21.

[5]*Ibid.*, 22-23.

[6]*Ibid.*

[7]*Ibid.*

[8]*Ibid.*

[9]*Ibid.*

[10]*Ibid.*

[11]*Ibid.*, 22.

[12]*Ibid.*

[13]*Ibid.*, 23.

[14]*Ibid.*

[15]Descendants of Nancy Jane Bevins Gragg Herndon, conversations with author, 1930s.

[16]*Ibid.*

[17]Dwane Meyer, *The History of Missouri* (Columbia: Missouri State Historical Society), 408.

[18]Descendants of Nancy Jane Bevins Gragg Herndon, conversations with author, 1930s.

[19]*Ibid.*

[20]*Ibid.*

[21]*Ibid.*; visit of author to location.

[22]*Ibid.*; study of maps by author.

[23]Descendants of Nancy Jane Bevins Gragg Herndon, conversations with author, 1940s.

[24]Muriel H. Wright, "David L. Payne and the Boomers," *The Story of Oklahoma* (Guthrie: Cooperative Publishing Company, date not clear), 238-242.

[25]*Ibid.*, Opal Hartsell Brown, "Trail Riding Pioneer Doctor," Orbit, *Daily Oklahoman and Times*, October 30, 1960, 22.

[26]Descendants of Nancy Jane Bevins Gragg Herndon, conversations with author, 1960s.

[27]Opal Hartsell Brown, "Trail Riding Pioneer Doctor," Orbit, *Daily Oklahoman and Times*, October 30, 1960, 22.

[28]*Ibid.*

[29]*Ibid.*; Glenn Shirley, *Belle Starr and Her Times* (Norman: University of Oklahoma Press, 1982), 233-234.

[30]Descendants of Nancy Jane Bevins Gragg Herndon, conversations with author, 1960s.

[31]*Ibid.*

[32]*Ibid.*

[33]*Ibid.*

[34]I.C. Gunning, *Royal Family of the Choctaws* (Eastern Oklahoma Historical Society, n.d.), 33, 39; Jo Reid, Descendant of Jane Austin McCurtain, conversation with author, 1992.

[35]I.C. Gunning, *Royal Family of the Choctaws*, 33, 39-40.

[36]*Ibid.*, 40.

[37]*Ibid.*, 37.

[38]*Ibid.*, 39.

[39]*Ibid.*

[40]*Ibid.*

[41]*Ibid.*

[42]*Ibid.*, 34.

[43]*Ibid.*, 41; Works Projects Administration of Oklahoma, *The WPA Guide to the 1930s Oklahoma*, 328.

[44]Angie Debo, *The Rise and Fall of the Choctaw Republic* (Norman: University of Oklahoma Press, 1934), 233.

[45]I.C. Gunning, *Royal Family of the Choctaws*, 42.

[46]Patti Russell, Descendant of Bessie Dink Edwards Chapman, interview with author, 1991; Opal Hartsell Brown, "Role Model in Spite of Age and Handicap," *Sulphur Times-Democrat*, April 25, 1991, 8A.

[47]*Ibid.*

[48]*Ibid.*

[49]*Ibid.*

[50]*Ibid.*

[51]Patti Russell and Carol Brown, descendants of Bessie Dink Edwards Chapman, paper on subject.

[52]*Ibid.*

[53]Opal Hartsell Brown, "Role Model in Spite of Age and Handicap," *Sulphur Times-Democrat*, April 25, 1991, 8A.

[54]*Ibid.*; Patti Russell, interview with author, 1991.

Chapter 3:

[1]Mary Bever, Descendant of Rhoda Pitchlynn Howell, "The Howell Family," in *Davis, Oklahoma*, ed. by Theresa Gabel (Oklahoma City: Western Heritage Books, 1981), 81.

[2]*Ibid.*, 84-85.

[3]*Ibid.*, Arbuckle Historical Societies of Davis and Sulphur, *Murray County II*, 331.

[4]Author Unlisted, "An Indian—A Leader for Half a Century," *Harlow's Weekly* (1920s); reprinted in Brown, *Murray County*, 309.

[5]Arbuckle Historical Societies of Davis and Sulphur, *Murray County II*, 331-332.

[6]Works Projects Administration, *The WPA Guide to 1930s Oklahoma*, 315.

[7]Francis L. and Roberta B. Fugate, *Roadside History of Oklahoma* (Missoula, Montana: Mountain Press), 98.

[8]Debo, *Rise and Fall of the Choctaw Republic*, 45, 177.

[9]*Ibid.*, 95-97.

[10]Mary Bever, "The Howell Family," in Gabel, ed., *Davis, Oklahoma*, 84.

[11]*Ibid.*

[12]*Ibid.*

[13]*Ibid.*

[14]*Ibid.*

[15]*Ibid.*; visit to site by author and interview with caretaker, 1992.

[16]Mary Bever, "The Howell Family," in Gabel, ed., *Davis, Oklahoma*, 84.

[17]Mary Bever, interview with author, 1992.

[18]"Grave Markers Give History Lessons," *Daily Oklahoman*, April 1950; reprinted in Brown, *Murray County*, 1977, 310.

[19]Jimy Earlene Brady Rose, *What God Hath Blessed*, ed. by Dot Atkins (Richardson, Texas: Rockwell International Printing Services Dept., 1976), 35, 50, 25.

[20]Jimy Earlene Brady Rose, interview with author, visits to ranches, 1993.

[21]*Ibid.*

[22]*Ibid.*

[23]Jimy Earlene Brady Rose, *What God Hath Blessed*, 23.

[24]*Ibid.*

[25]*Ibid.*, 23-24.

[26]*Ibid.*

[27]*Ibid.*, 27.

[28]*Ibid.*, 77.

[29]*Ibid.*, 77-78, 81.

[30]*Ibid.*, 8-9, 102.

[31]*Ibid.*, 100-101.

[32]*Ibid.*, 82.

[33]*Ibid.*, 126.

[34]*Ibid.*, 123.

[35]*Ibid.*

[36]*Ibid.*, 135.

[37]*Ibid.*

[38]*Ibid.*

[39]*Ibid.*, 81.

[40]*Ibid.*, 82.

[41]*Ibid.*, 35.

[42]*Ibid.*

[43]*Ibid.*

[44]*Ibid.*, *38, 46.*

[45]*Ibid.*, 38.

[46]*Ibid.*

[47]*Ibid.*

[48]*Ibid.*, 81.

[49]*Ibid.*; "Jimy Brady Rose to Sizzle," *Daily Ardmoreite*, September 7, 1981.

[50]*Ibid.*

[51]*Ibid.*

[52]Mary Ann James, telephone conversation with author, 1988; letter to author, 1988.

[53]Works Projects Administration, *The WPA Guide to 1930s Oklahoma*, 332.

[54]Opal Hartsell Brown, "Sooner Footprints," *Sulphur Times-Democrat*, September 8, 1988.

[55]*Ibid.*

[56]*Ibid.*

[57]Mary Ann James, telephone conversation with author, 1993.

Chapter 4:

[1]Hugh D. Corwin, *Comanche and Kiowa Captives in Oklahoma and Texas* (Guthrie: Cooperative Publishing Company, 1959), 97.

[2]*Ibid.*, 7, 11.

[3]*Ibid.*

[4]*Ibid.*, 11.

[5]*Ibid.*, 7.

[6]*Ibid.*, 8.

[7]*Ibid.*, 8, 12.

[8]*Ibid.*, 12.

[9]*Ibid.*, 9.

[10]*Ibid.*, 8-9.

[11]*Ibid.*, 97.

[12]*Ibid.*, 105.

[13]Muriel H. Wright, *A Guide to the Indian Tribes of Oklahoma* (Norman: University of Oklahoma Press, 1951), 34.

[14]Corwin, *Comanches and Kiowa Captives*, 106.

[15]*Ibid.*

[16]*Ibid.*, 106-107.

[17]*Ibid.*, 107.

[18]*Ibid.*, 108.

[19]*Ibid.*, 109.

[20]*Ibid.*

[21]*Ibid.*; Hugh D. Corwin, *The Kiowa Indians—Their History and Life Stories* (1958), 50.

[22]Corwin, *Comanches and Kiowa Captives*, 117.

[23]*Ibid.*, 117-121.

[24]Opal Hartsell Brown, "Wild Old Days — Cinderella of the Captives," *True West* (July 1982), 56.

[25]*Ibid.*

[26]*Ibid.*

[27]*Ibid.*

[28]*Ibid.*, 56-57.

[29]*Ibid.*, 57.

[30]*Ibid.*

[31]*Ibid.*

[32]*Ibid.*

[33]Brown, "Wild Old Days," 57-59.
[34]*Ibid.*
[35]*Ibid.*
[36]Corwin, *Comanches and Kiowa Captives*, 120-121.
[37]*Ibid.*, 121; Brown, "Wild Old Days," 57.
[38]Waco (Texas) Census, July 5, 1870.
[39]Brown, "Wild Old Days," 57.
[40]*Ibid.*
[41]Brown, "Wild Old Days," 57.
[42]*Ibid.*
[43]*Ibid.*, 58.
[44]*Ibid.*
[45]*Ibid.*
[46]*Ibid.*
[47]Herta Huge Bohm Lucas, interview with author, July, 1990.
[48]*Ibid.*
[49]Opal Hartsell Brown, "Transplanted Oklahoman Caught in European Crossfire," *Sulphur Times-Democrat*, October 18, 1990, 18.
[50]*Ibid.*
[51]*Ibid.*
[52]Herta Huge Bohm Lucas, "Courage—Portrait of a Woman's Survival" (unpublished autobiography), 5-10.
[53]*Ibid.*
[54]Herta Huge Bohm Lucas, interview with author, 1990.
[55]*Ibid.*
[56]Herta Huge Bohm Lucas, interview with author, 1990.
[58]*Ibid.*
[59]*Ibid.*

Chapter 5:

[1]Mildred Imache Cleghorn, interview with author, 1991; personal observation of Cleghorn on television, 1992, Others.
[2]Fort-Sill Apache Agency, Résumé, Mildred Imache Cleghorn.
[3]Mildred Imache Cleghorn, interview with author, 1991.
[4]*Ibid.*
[5]Oklahoma Education Association, "OREA News Bulletin," September 30, 1990; Southwest Oklahoma Genealogical Society, *Comanche County*, 16.
[6]*Ibid.*
[7]*Ibid.*
[8]Oklahoma Education Association, "OREA News Bulletin," September 30, 1990.
[9]*Ibid.*; Mildred Imache Cleghorn, interview with author, 1991.
[10]*Ibid.*
[11]*Ibid.*
[12]*Ibid.*
[13]*Ibid.*
[14]*Ibid.*
[15]*Ibid.*; Oklahoma Education Association, "OREA News Bulletin," September 30, 1990.
[16]Mildred Imache Cleghorn, interview with author; personal observation of subject on Smithsonian Institution program, 1992.
[17]Mildred Imache Cleghorn, interview with author, 1991.
[18]"Geronimo," *National Geographic* (October 1992), 68-69.
[19]Mildred Imache Cleghorn, interview with author, 1991.
[20]*Ibid.*
[21]*Ibid.*
[22]Mrs. W.S. Key, "A Tribute to Alice Brown Davis," *Chronicles of Oklahoma*, 43, 97; Opal Hartsell Brown, "Sooner Footprints," *Sulphur Times-Democrat*, January 15, 1987, 12A.
[23]Carolyn Foreman, *Indian Women Chiefs*, 63-64.
[24]Key, "Tribute to Alice Brown Davis," 43, 97.
[25]*Ibid.*
[26]Charles W. Mooney, *Localized History of Pottawatomie County, Oklahoma to 1907* (1971), 37.
[27]*Ibid.*
[28]*Ibid.*
[29]Wright, *Story of Oklahoma*, 166-167.
[30]Mooney, *Localized History of Pottawatomie County*, 37.
[31]Foreman, *Indian Women Chiefs*, 64.
[32]*Ibid.*; Brown, "Sooner Footprints."
[33]*Ibid.*

[34]Foreman, *Indian Women Chiefs*, 64.
[35]*Ibid.*
[36]*Ibid.*; Key, "Tribute to Alice Brown Davis," 43, 97.
[37]Thomas Wildcat Alcord, as told to Florence Drake, *Civilization and the Story of the Absentee Shawnees* (Norman: University of Oklahoma Press, 1979), 187-199; Mooney, *Localized History of Pottawatomie County*, 306.
[38]*Ibid.*; Foreman, *Indian Women Chiefs*, 60-61.
[39]*Ibid.*
[40]Mooney, *Localized History of Pottawatomie County*, 307.
[41]*Ibid.*
[42]*Ibid.*
[43]*Ibid.*; Wright, *Guide to the Indian Tribes of Oklahoma*, 168; she spelled the chief's name "Wah-Poho-ko, wah."
[44]*Ibid.*
[45]*Ibid.*
[46]Author Unknown, *The Tribal System Political and Legal Organization*, 108-109.
[47]Wright, *Guide to the Indian Tribes of Oklahoma*, 168.
[48]Alcord, *Civilization and the Story of the Absentee Shawnees*, 162, 169, 171, 189.
[49]*Ibid.*
[50]*Ibid.*, 171, 173.
[51]*Ibid.*, 177.
[52]*Ibid.*, 181, 187.
[53]*Ibid.*, 188-189.
[54]*Ibid.*, 189.
[55]*Ibid.*, 190.
[56]Foreman, *Indian Women Chiefs*, 61.
[57]*Ibid.*, 59.
[58]"Chief of the Cherokees," *Southern Living*, 190; Electronic and Printed Media of 1993, News Stories, Public Information of 1993.
[59]Michale Wallace, "A History-Wilma Mankiller" (Manuscript, 1988), 68.
[60]*Ibid.*
[61]Rod Davis, "Trail of Triumph," *American Way* (January 15, 1988), 61.
[62]"Women in the Workplace," Southwestern Bell Corporation Update, No. 1, 1989, 50 (brochure)
[63]Davis, "Trail of Triumph," 61.
[64]*Ibid.*; visits to area by author.
[65]Davis, "Trail of Triumph," 61.
[66]Marilyn Bell, "Chief Mankiller: How a Life Relates to Cherokee Nation Goals," *Oklahoma Rural News* (August 1991), 10.
[67]Davis, "Trail of Triumph," 61.
[68]*Ibid.*
[69]*Ibid.*; "Cherokee Nation Communications," Tahlequah.
[70]Bell, "Chief Mankiller," 10; "Chief of the Cherokees," *Southern Living* (date not legible), 190.
[71]*Ibid.*
[72]Davis, "Trail of Triumph," 61.
[73]*Ibid.*, 62.
[74]Marilyn Awiakta, "The Turning Point," *Southern Style* (September-October, year and page not legible).
[75]*Ibid.*
[76]*Ibid.*
[77]"Cherokee Nation Communication."
[78]*Ibid.*
[79]*Ibid.*
[80]*Ibid.*
[81]Davis, "Trail of Triumph," 101.
[82]*Ibid.*
[83]Bell, "Chief Mankiller," 10.
[84]Personal observations, copies of publications in hand.

Chapter 6

[1]Corwin, *The Kiowa Indians*, 113, 119.
[2]*Ibid.*, 121.
[3]*Ibid.*
[4]*Ibid.*
[5]*Ibid.*, 120.
[6]Author's knowledge.

[7]Corwin, *The Kiowa Indians*, 120.

[8]*Ibid.*, 128.

[9]*Ibid.*, 130.

[10]*Ibid.*

[11]*Ibid.*, 131.

[12]Pete A. Becker, "Post Oak Mission," *Prairie Lore*, Southwest Oklahoma Historical Society (October 1975), 111; Opal Hartsell Brown, "Russian Refugee-Missionary to the Indians," *Prairie Lore* (April 1976), 226.

[13]Brown, "Russian Refugee," 227.

[14]*Ibid.*; Anna Hiebert Gomez, interview with author, 1950s.

[15]*Ibid.*

[16]*Ibid.*

[17]*Ibid.*; Brown, "Russian Refugee," 228.

[18]*Ibid.*

[19]*Ibid.*, 229.

[20]*Ibid.*, 227.

[21]Anna Hiebert Gomez, interview with author, 1950s.

[22]*Ibid.*

[23]*Ibid.*; Brown, "Russian Refugee," 226.

[24]*Ibid.*

[25]*Ibid.*

[26]*Ibid.*

[27]Anna Klyde Bennett Davis, interviews with author, 1965-1966.

[28]"A Former Lawtonian, Malaysian Missionary Worker Visiting Here," *Lawton Constitution*, August 29, 1968, 14.

[29]Anna Klyde Bennett Davis, interviews with author, 1968.

[30]*Ibid.*

[31]*Ibid.*

[32]*Ibid.*

[33]*Ibid.*

[34]"A Former Lawtonian, Malaysian Missionary Worker Visiting Here," *Lawton Constitution*, August 29, 1968, 14.

[35]Anna Klyde Bennett Davis, interviews with author, 1967-1968.

[36]*Ibid.*

[37]"A Former Lawtonian, Malaysian Missionary Worker Visiting Here," *Lawton Constitution*, August 29, 1968, 14.

[38]Anna Klyde Bennett Davis, interviews with author, 1968.

[39]*Ibid.*

[40]Anna Klyde Bennett Davis, lectures, Church of Christ, Lawton, 1968.

[41]*Ibid.*

[42]*Ibid.*

[43]Anna Klyde Bennett Davis, interviews with author, 1969-1971.

[44]Anna Klyde Bennett Davis, letters to author, 1968-1969.

[45]Author attended memorial services for Anna Klyde Bennett Davis, Church of Christ, Shawnee, Oklahoma, 1982.

[46]Louise Davis McMahan, *Reminiscences and Scrap Book* (McMahan Foundation, 1957), 135.

[47]Louise Davis McMahan, "Remembrances of Lawton's Early Days," *Prairie Lore*, Southwest Oklahoma Historical Society (January 1977), 185.

[48]Jennie L. McCutcheon, "The McMahan Foundation," in *Reminiscences and Scrap Book*, 132-144.

[49]*Ibid.*

[50]McMahan, *Reminiscences and Scrap Book*, 64-65.

[51]*Ibid.*, 132, 145.

[52]*Ibid.*, 2, 196.

[53]*Ibid.*, 3-4.

[54]*Ibid.*, 93.

[55]*Ibid.*, 10-11, 18.

[56]*Ibid.*, 20-21.

[57]*Ibid.*, 21.

[58]*Ibid.*, 21-22.

[59]*Ibid.*, 22-23.

[60]*Ibid.*, 25-26.

[61]*Ibid.*, 27-28.

[62]*Ibid.*, 29-30, 40.

[63]*Ibid.*, 31, 41.

[64]*Ibid.*, 185, 187.

[65]*Ibid.*

[66]Jennie L. McCutcheon, "Five Years With Mrs. McMahan," in *Reminiscences and Scrap Book*, 145.

[67]McMahan, *Reminiscences and Scrap Book*, 52-53.

[68]*Ibid.*, 53.

[69]*Ibid.*, 54, 57.

[70]*Ibid.*, 58-59, 123, 64.

[71]Mrs. Edgar Deen, Letter, in McMahan, *Reminiscences and Scrap Book*, 124-126.

[72]McMahan, *Reminiscences and Scrap Book*, 125, 142-144.

[73]McCutcheon, "Five Years With Mrs. McMahan," in McMahan, *Reminiscences and Scrap Book*, 149.

[74]Visits to McMahan Media Center, Lawton Public Schools, Lawton, Oklahoma.

Chapter 7:

[1]Editorial Offices, "Official Biography—Eleanor M. (West) Johnson," *Weekly Reader* (Connecticut, 1991), 1.

[2]Durwood Newsom, *Drumright! The Glory Days of a Boom Town*, 149.

[3]"Official Biography—Eleanor M. (West) Johnson," 1.

[4]*Ibid.*

[5]*Ibid.*

[6]Terry Borton, Vice-president and Editor in Chief, *Weekly Reader*, letter to author, 1992.

[7]"Official Biography-Eleanor M. (West) Johnson," 2.

[8]Newsom, *Drumright!*, 149.

[9]"Official Biography-Eleanor M. (West) Johnson," 2.

[10]*Ibid.*

[11]Eleanor M. (West) Johnson, letter to Janice Skene, 1986.

[12]*Ibid.*

[13]Editorial Offices, *Weekly Reader*, December 4, 1987.

[14]J. Harold Crosby, "Jeanette Smith Crosby, Lawton Pioneer," *Prairie Lore*, Southwest Oklahoma Historical Society (July 1973), 16.

[15]*Ibid.*

[16]*Ibid.*

[17]Genevieve Crosby Rehkopf, "Jeanette Smith Crosby, a Remarkable Woman," *Prairie Lore*, Southwest Oklahoma Historical Society (October 1979), 85.

[18]Crosby, "Jeanette Smith Crosby, Lawton Pioneer," 17.

[19]*Ibid.*

[20]Rehkopf, "Jeanette Smith Crosby, a Remarkable Woman," 88.

[21]*Ibid.*, 89, 90.

[22]*Standard American Encyclopedia* XIII, unnumbered; visit to location by author, 1950s.

[23]Crosby, "Jeanette Smith Crosby, Lawton Pioneer," 16.

[24]Rehkopf, "Jeanette Smith Crosby, a Remarkable Woman," 90.

[25]*Ibid.*, 85.

[26]*Ibid.*, 90.

[27]Lucille Taylor Pintz, interview with author, 1989; Opal Hartsell Brown, "Sulphur Woman, Progenitor of Head Start," *Sulphur Times-Democrat*, November 16, 1989, 12B.

[28]*Ibid.*

[29]*Ibid.*

[30]*Ibid.*

[31]Lucille Taylor Pintz, Program for Arbuckle Historical Society, Sulphur, 1988.

[32]"BPW Names Lucille Pintz 'Sulphur Woman of the Year,'" *Sulphur Times-Democrat*, October 24, 1991, 7A.

[33]Brown, "Sulphur Woman, Progenitor of Head Start."

[34]*Ibid.*

[35]*Ibid.*

[36]Lucille Taylor Pintz, interviews with author, 1989-1990.

[37]*Ibid.*

[38]Brown, "Sulphur Woman, Progenitor of Head Start."

[39]*Ibid.*

[40]*Ibid.*

[41]"New Lawyer in the West," publisher unlisted, Archives, Pauls Valley Memorial Library, Pauls Valley, 1991.

[42]*Ibid.*

[43]*Ibid.*

[44]*Ibid.*

[45]*Standard American Encyclopedia*, XIII, n.p.

[46]Sara Thomason, "Necrology, Anabel Fleming Thomason,"

Chronicles of Oklahoma, 499-500.

47"New Lawyer in the West," 3.

48*Ibid.*, 4.

49Visits to site by author.

50Thomason, "Necrology Anabel Fleming Thomason," 499.

51"New Lawyer in the West," 3.

52Thomason, "Necrology, Anabel Fleming Thomason," 499-500.

53Media coverage of subject viewed by author, 1967-1992.

54Miss America Pageant, Atlantic City, New Jersey, 1967, viewed by author on television.

55*Ibid.*

56Donita Lucas Shields, "America's Ideal Young Woman: Jane Jayroe, Pride of Western Oklahoma," *Westview* (Weatherford: Southwest Oklahoma State University, Spring 1986), 5.

57Michelle Nalley, KOCO-TV, 5 Alive, Oklahoma City, "Jayroe 5 Alive Anchor"; letter to author, 1990.

58Shields, "America's Ideal Young Woman," 6.

59Public Relations Department, KOCO-TV, "Jane Jayroe, Vita," 1990.

60*Ibid.*

61*Ibid.*

62Reports from observers to author.

63Shields, "America's Ideal Young Woman," 6.

64*Ibid.*

65*Ibid.*

66Public Relations Department, KOCO-TV, "Jane Jayroe, Vita," 1990.

67Bernice Love, "Three State Beauties Bring Home Miss America Crown," *Daily Oklahoman*, November 15, 1987, 8.

68*Ibid.*

69Linda Miller, "Roller Coaster Life Plagues Anita Bryant," *Daily Oklahoman*, November 15, 1987, 9D.

70*Ibid.*

71Descendants of Mollie Colbert, Penner Ranch, Mill Creek, Oklahoma, interview with author, 1990; Opal Hartsell Brown, "Penner Ranch Outgrowth of Old Mill Creek," *Sulphur Times-Democrat*, December 13, 1990, 6A.

Chapter 8:

1Irene Sturm Lefebvre, interview with author, 1990.

2*Ibid.*

3*Pictorial History of the Second World War*, II (New York: William H. Wise, 1949), 650-651.

4Irene Sturm Lefebvre, interview with author, 1990.

5*Ibid.*

6*Ibid.*

7*Ibid.*

8*Pictorial History of the Second World War*, II, 650-651.

9Irene Sturm Lefebvre, interview with author, 1990; *Standard American Encyclopedia*, IV, 2015-2022.

10Irene Sturm Lefebvre, interview with author, 1990.

11Irene Sturm Lefebvre, ed., *Brand Book, Women's Posse of Oklahoma Westerners*, 1980s.

12*Ibid.*

13*Ibid.*

14*Ibid.*

15*Ibid.*

16"Oklahoma Authors," *Daily Oklahoman*, Book Page, 1992, 1.

17*Ibid.*; Lefebvre, ed., *Brand Book*, 1-3.

18Irene Sturm Lefebvre, letter to author, 1990.

19*Ibid.*

20Johnnie Lee Pennington, interview with author, 1990; Opal Hartsell Brown, "Sulphur Woman Left Footprints Around the World," *Sulphur Times-Democrat*, September 20, 1990, 10A.

21*Ibid.*

22*Ibid.*

23*Ibid.*; Johnnie Lee Pennington, Program, Arbuckle Historical Society of Sulphur, 1989.

24*Ibid.*

25*Ibid.*

26Johnnie Lee Pennington, Vita, 1990.

27*Ibid.*

28Brown, "Sulphur Woman Left Footprints Around the World."

29*Ibid.*

30*Ibid.*

31Helen Freudenberger Holmes, "Data," 1990.

32*Ibid.*

33Helen Freudenberger Holmes, Program, Oklahoma City Branch, National League of American Pen Women, 1989.

34*Pictorial History of the Second World War*, II, William H. Wise, 618-640.

35Helen Freudenberger Holmes, "Data," 1990.

36*Ibid.*

37*Ibid.*

38*Ibid.*

39*Ibid.*; Helen Freudenberger Holmes, Program, Oklahoma City Branch, National League of American Pen Women, 1989.

40Helen Freudenberger Holmes, "Data," 1990.

41Nellie Belle Blackard Horsman, interviews with author, 1988-1990.

42Opal Hartsell Brown, "Military Wives Heroic in War or Peace," *Sulphur Times-Democrat*, January 25, 1990, 8A.

43*Ibid.*

44*Ibid.*

45*Ibid.*; Nellie Belle Blackard Horsman, interviews with author, 1988-1993.

46*Ibid.*

47*Ibid.*; Brown, "Military Wives Heroic in War or Peace."

48*Ibid.*

49*Ibid.*

50Nellie Belle Blackard Horsman, personal contacts, 1989-1993.

51*Ibid.*

52*Ibid.*

53*Ibid.*

54Brown, "Military Wives Heroic in War or Peace."

55*Ibid.*

56Nellie Belle Blackard Horsman, personal contacts, 1989-1993.

57*Ibid.*

58Brown, "Military Wives Heroic in War or Peace."

59Exodus 15:20, and Matthew 14:6-11, Bible.

Chapter 9:

1Works Projects Administration, *The WPA Guide to 1930s Oklahoma*, 105-106.

2*Ibid.*

3Author and title unknown, Chapter 5, "Swing Low, Sweet Chariot, Dedicated to the Memory of My Friend, Mrs. Jimmie Kirby, granddaughter of Britt Willis, the Man Who Owned the Talented Slaves, Uncle Wallace and Aunt Minerva," 15.

4*Ibid.*, 16.

5*Ibid.*, 15.

6*Ibid.*

7*Ibid.*

8*Ibid.*; Works Projects Administration, *The WPA Guide to 1930s Oklahoma*, 106.

9Tsianina, *Where Trails Have Led Me* (Santa Fe, New Mexico: N.p., 1968), 7-143.

10*Ibid.*

11*Ibid.*, 7.

12*Ibid.*, 8, 15, 10.

13*Ibid.*, 9, 13.

14*Ibid.*; James M. Etter, *Oktaha, A Track in the Sand* (Oktaha: Oktaha Historical Society), 189.

15Tsianina, *Where Trails Have Led Me*, 20-22.

16*Ibid.*, 25-28.

17*Ibid.*, 53-62, 118-123.

18*Ibid.*, "Introduction," *Dictionary of Musicians*, 88.

19Tsianina, *Where Trails Have Led Me*, 87.

20*Ibid.*, 87, 92.

21*Ibid.*, 89-90.

22*Ibid.*, 89-96, 103.

23*Ibid.*, 108-109, 127.

24*Ibid.*

25*Ibid.*, 15, 133-135.

[26]*Ibid.*, 107.

[27]"Te Ata," Introduction and Program of Subject's Engagements, Courtesy Chickasaw Nation Museum, Tishomingo, 1990.

[28]*Ibid.*

[29]Employees, Chickasaw Nation Museum, Tishomingo, 1991; Ann De Frange, "Te Ata's Unique Way Makes Her A 'Treasure,'" *Daily Oklahoman*, September 13, 1987, 1.

[30]*Ibid.*

[31]Lee Millhouse, "Te Ata, Chickasaw Storyteller," *Prairie Lore*, Southwest Oklahoma Historical Society (October 1989), 90.

[32]"Te Ata," Chickasaw Nation Museum, Tishomingo, 1990.

[33]"Chickasaw Cultural Center to Host Author's Signing Party and Reception," *Sulphur Times-Democrat*, April 5, 1990.

[34]"Te Ata," Chickasaw Nation Museum, Tishomingo, 1990.

[35]DeFrange, "Te Ata's Unique Way Makes Her a Treasure, 1.

[36]*Ibid.*

[37]"Te Ata," Chickasaw Nation Museum, Tishomingo, 1990.

[38]De Frange, "Te Ata's Unique Way Makes Her a 'Treasure.'"

[39]*Ibid.*

[40]Millhouse, "Te Ata, Chickasaw Storyteller," 90.

[41]"Chickasaw Cultural Center to Host Author's Signing Party and Reception."

[42]Personal acquaintance with Boren-Axton families since the 1930s.

[43]Ellie Posey, "Former Sooner Isn't Lacking in Recognition," *Daily Oklahoman*, date unavailable.

[44]Mae Boren Axton, conversations with author since 1930s.

[45]*Ibid.*

[46]*Ibid.*

[47]*Ibid.*

[48]Mae Boren Axton, "An Overview," 1993, 1.

[49]*Ibid.*

[50]*Ibid.*; Mae Boren Axton, letters to author, 1993.

[51]*Ibid.*

[52]*Ibid.*

[53]Hoyt Axton, "Press Release, 1993," 2.

[54]*Ibid.*

[55]*Ibid.*, 4.

[56]*Ibid.*, 3-4..

[57]Mae Boren Axton, communications with author; "A Tribute to Mae Boren Axton," *Congressional Record*, February 3, 1988.

[58]Axton, "An Overview," 1993.

[59]*Ibid.*

[60]*Ibid.*; "A Tribute to Mae Boren Axton," *Congressional Record*, February 3, 1989.

[61]*Ibid.*; Posey, "Former Sooner Isn't Lacking in Recognition."

[62]Axton, "An Overview," 1993.

[63]Comments by friends of Mae Boren Axton.

[64]Mae Boren Axton, conversations with author on various occasions.

[65]*Ibid.*

Chapter 10:

[1]George and Louise Dale Nelson, interview with author, 1975.

[2]*Ibid.*; personal association, 1970s.

[3]Louise Dale Nelson, *When the Heart Speaks* (Mountain Park, Ok.: Trumpet Vine Press, 1968).

[4]Louise Dale Nelson, interviews with author, 1976.

[5]Nelson, *When the Heart Speaks*.

[6]*Ibid.*

[7]George and Louise Dale Nelson, interviews with author, 1976.

[8]Opal Hartsell Brown, "Making Book on the Good Life, NRTA Notables," *NRTA Journal* (July-August 1976), 16.

[9]George and Louise Dale Nelson, conversations with author, 1976.

[10]Opal Hartsell Brown, "Ingenuity Part of Home," *Sunday Magazine of the Wichita Falls Times*, January 25, 1976, 2.

[11]George and Louise Dale Nelson, conversations with author, 1975.

[12]*Ibid.*

[13]*Ibid.*

[14]*Ibid.*

[15]George and Louise Dale Nelson, Program presented to Great Plains Writers, Lawton, 1976.

[16]*Ibid.*

[17]Book in author's possession.

[18]Jennie Harris Oliver, personal acquaintance of author.

[19]Mary Hays Marable and Elaine Boylan, *A Handbook of Oklahoma Writers* (Norman: University of Oklahoma Press, 1939), 25.

[20]*Ibid.*

[21]*Ibid.*, 26.

[22]Author's visit to site, 1938; Census Report, *Daily Oklahoman*, January 28, 1991, 6.

[23]Marable and Boylan, *Handbook of Oklahoma Writers*, 26-27.

[24]*Ibid.*

[25]*Ibid.*, 28.

[26]Jennie Harris Oliver, Program, Oklahoma State Writers, Oklahoma City, 1939.

[27]Marable and Boylan, *Handbook of Oklahoma Writers*, 26-27.

[28]*Ibid.*

[29]Author in attendance; Joe Fitzpatrick and Jennie Harris Oliver, "Here Rests Thy Caravan," *The Singing Hand of Joe Fitzpatrick* (Publisher and date unavailable).

[30]Book in author's possession.

[31]"Mrs. Oliver's Latest Story Is Inspired by City Singer," *Daily Oklahoman*, date unknown, but in 1930s.

[32]Author attended event, 1939.

[33]Linnie Mae Schultz (deceased), Oklahoma City, member of Literary Club, 1938-1939.

[34]*Ibid.*

[35]Adrienne Cochran Huey, interviews with author, 1990-1992.

[36]Adrienne Cochran Huey, letters to author, 1993.

[37]*Ibid.*

[38]Adrienne Cochran Huey, *The Journal of Foreign Service* (N.p., n.d.).

[39]*Ibid.*

[40]*Ibid.*

[41]*Ibid.*

[42]Adrienne Cochran Huey, letters to author, 1992-1993.

[43]Huey, *The Journal of Foreign Service*.

[44]*Ibid.*

[45]*Ibid.*

[46]Adrienne Cochran Huey, conversations with author, 1991-1992.

[47]Huey, *The Journal of Foreign Service*.

[48]*Ibid.*

[49]Adrienne Cochran Huey, Vita, 1992.

[50]*Ibid.*

[51]*Ibid.*

[52]*Ibid.*

[53]Adrienne Cochran Huey, letter to author.

[54]*Ibid.*

Chapter 11:

[1]Edna Miller Hennessee, guided author on tour of plant, 1992.

[2]*Ibid.*

[3]*Ibid.*

[4]Author's visit to Malaysia, 1962.

[5]Author's knowledge from experience.

[6]Edna Miller Hennessee, personal acquaintance and conversations with author, 1949-1990.

[7]Edna Miller Hennessee, Vita, 1991.

[8]*Ibid.*

[9]Edna Miller Hennessee, acquaintance and conversation with author, 1949-1990.

[10]*Ibid.*

[11]*Ibid.*

[12]*Ibid.*

[13]Edna Miller Hennessee, Vita, 1991.

[14]Edna Miller Hennessee, acquaintance and conversation with Author.

[15]*Ibid.*, Vita.

[16]*Ibid.*

[17]*Ibid.*

[18]Author's prior knowledge.

[19]Mollie Sue Levite Griffis, Vita.

[20]Mollie Sue Levite Griffis, letter to author.

[21]*Ibid.*

[22]"Apache, Oklahoma," (booklet, about 1908), 1-26.

[23]*Ibid.*

[24]George Levite, *By George, for Lilly* (Norman: M & L Publisher, 1986), 1-60.

[25]*Ibid.*

[26]*Ibid.*, 29, 44, 18, 23.

[27]*Ibid.*, 27-28.

[28]Mollie Sue Levite Griffis, conversations with author, 1991.

[29]Kim McConnell, "Apache Publisher Gets Addition to Old Book," *Lawton Constitution*, December 26, 1992, 3A; Mollie Sue Levite Griffis, letter to author, 1991.

[30]Mollie Sue Levite Griffis, Program for Pen Women, Oklahoma City, 1990.

[31]J.E. McReynolds, "Small Publisher Builds on Solid Foundation," *Daily Oklahoman*, Business Section, June 4, 1989, 2.

[32]Mollie Sue Levite Griffis, conversation with and letter to author, 1991.

[33]Mollie Sue Levite Griffis, Vita, 1991.

[34]*Ibid.*

[35]Frankie Sue Gage Gilliam, letter to author, 1992.

[36]*Ibid.*

[37]Copy of *Twin Territories* in hand.

[38]Frankie Sue Gage Gilliam, Vita.

[39]Frankie Sue Gage Gilliam, letter to author; Vita.

[40]*Ibid.*

[41]*Ibid.*

[42]*Ibid.*

[43]Frankie Sue Gage Gilliam, letter to author, 1992.

[44]"Muskogee Paper Celebrates Oklahoma Heritage," *Current* (January/February 1991), 1-3.

[45]*Ibid.*

[46]*Ibid.*, 1.

[47]*Ibid.*, 2.

[48]Joan Morrison, "Proud Okie Always Knew She'd Pursue Career in Tourism," *Muskogee Daily Phoenix*, November 16, 1992, 1A.

[49]*Ibid.*, 8A.

[50]"Muskogee Paper Celebrates Oklahoma Heritage."

[51]Frankie Sue Gage Gilliam, letter and brochure to author, 1992.

[52]Visit to site by author, 1988.

[53]Jane Miller Hardin, conversations with author, 1978-1993.

[54]Better Business Bureau of Central Oklahoma, Inc., "Biography, Jane Miller Hardin," 1992, 1-3.

[55]*Ibid.*

[56]Jane Miller Hardin, interviews and conversations with author, 1978-1993.

[57]Better Business Bureau, "Biography, Jane Miller Hardin," 1-3.

[58]*Ibid.*

[59]*Ibid.*

[60]Ken Hardin, Better Business Bureau of Central Oklahoma, Inc., conversations with author, 1983-1986.

[61]Jane Miller Hardin, interview with author, 1991.

[62]Visits to Bureau by author.

[63]Jane Miller Hardin, interview with author.

[64]*Ibid.*

[65]*Ibid.*

[66]Better Business Bureau, "Biography, Jane Miller Hardin," 1-2.

[67]Jane Miller Hardin, interview with author, 1992.

[68]*Ibid.*

[69]*Standard American Encyclopedia*, IX, n.p.

[70]Debo, *Rise and Fall of the Choctaw Republic*, 9-10, 18, 77, 232-233.

[71]Dorothy Milligan, ed., *The Indian Way—Chickasaws* (Wichita Falls: Nortex Press, 1976), 44-46, 79; Milligan, *The Indian Way—The Choctaws*, 101-107.

Chapter 12:

[1]Bernice Norman Crockett, "No Job for a Woman," *Chronicles of Oklahoma*, 148-163.

[2]*Ibid.*, 149.

[3]*Ibid.*, 152.

[4]*Ibid.*, 154.

[5]*Ibid.*

[6]*Ibid.*

INDEX